PLANTING SEEDS

FOR

HAPPINESS

LEARNING TO TRUST YOUR INTUITION
AND GROW YOUR TRUE SELF

Published in Canada, for Global Distribution by YGTMedia Co. www.ygtmedia.co/publishing

To order additional copies of this book: publishing@ygtmedia.co

Edited by Kelly Lamb

Interior design and typesetting by Doris Chung

Cover design by Michelle Fairbanks

eBook by Ellie Sipilä

Author Photo by Micaela Cali

PLANTING SEEDS

FOR

HAPPINESS

LEARNING TO TRUST YOUR INTUITION AND GROW YOUR TRUE SELF

NATALIA HARHAJ

THIS BOOK IS DEDICATED TO PREVIOUS GENERATIONS AND THE FAMILY MEMBERS WHO TOLD US ABOUT THEIR INNER KNOWING: ANNA PALYNSKA, MARIA HARHAJ, STEFAN HARHAJ, AND MY GODMOTHER. YOU HELPED US FIND OURS.

POEMS

INTRODUCTION

BEGINNING THE JOURNEY

*W*ho am I? At some point in one's life, this question is asked. Usually the pondering of one's meaning, of one's identity, corresponds to a major life milestone, especially a birth or a death. For me, this question lingered after the birth of my first child. I was on maternity leave and dealing with a newborn. Suddenly my life seemed different. I seemed different. Between sleep deprivation, breastfeeding, diaper changes, and everything else that became my new normal over-night, I was questioning the meaning of my life. What did I really want out of my one life? Why was I doing all of this? What was I missing by not being present and chasing the future? I struggled. I was exhausted and angry. I didn't know who I was, what I wanted, and how to take care of myself. I did everything to keep him fed, dry, cared for, and my cup was empty. I had little to offer myself and others because I did not know how to fill my cup back up. In this book, I explore the meaning of your life and how to keep your cup full.

I had internal conflict, which bubbled over into the relationships closest to me. I was exhausted, I could not find my grounded self because I wasn't grounded to begin with, which led to regular conflict around me. Losing my temper with everyone, near and far. I felt that no matter where I went the conflict came with me. Now I acknowledge it was within me and no one else. I was creating a new space for myself without realizing that it could be easy. I was making it challenging and seeing it as being harder than it really was. I was resisting the changes. I was fighting for a different reality than I was in. I was thinking about my old reality—my pre-baby reality—and trying to keep that, but it no longer fit into this new situation. I could not go back. I had to find inner peace to really embrace the changes and newness of all of this. Prior to motherhood, I didn't know how to give myself time to heal by asking or accepting help. I had to figure it out on my own. That was unnecessarily challenging because I needed help in order to give myself time to heal.

This book is the learnings I collected throughout my journey as a woman finding herself during a major life transition. I walk you through what I learned during that time with my new baby, my new life. I learned what I wanted for myself. This book is a journey of a mother and what she learned along the way to better herself and live a joyful life of opportunity and being present. It's for any woman experiencing a major life transition that results in them questioning themselves and exploring their intuition. **One thing I've learned through my journey is that our true self is deep within each of us.** Usually, we've been too afraid to let her fully come out. To fully be seen. This book is for any woman looking for a hand of support as they inspire themselves in their everyday tasks.

I know you are filled with all the skills, ideas, and potential you need. You need the confidence to unleash your potential. This book is for you—and I'm here to tell you that I see you and cannot wait for you to lean into all of it. It's not about completion, it's about the journey. And this book is about the beginning of my journey, which will hopefully spark your own journey. It's about moving forward with intention. You have been given the opportunity to do something with your life.

There are three ways to authentically be connected to yourself and who you are:

1. **Being rooted in yourself.** Being you, deep down you.
   - What brings you joy?
   - What is *your* purpose, beyond any role?
   - What does your voice sound like?

2. **Living a life of creation.** Make time to create and discover. Explore:
   - Your creativity
   - Gaining a new perspective
   - Uncovering your path
3. **Remembering you are alive.** With that comes the opportunity to use your time wisely. Honor the fact that:
   - You are a piece of it all
   - You are here today
   - Your time is important

This book is here to give you space to be yourself and to plant seeds for the years to come. To plant seeds today. It is to help you dream bigger and at the same time, to be more present in the current moment. I hold space for you to find exactly what you are looking for. You are the only one who knows what that looks like for you. Embrace the journey, embrace the unknown. There is much to discover when you do not need to have all the answers right away. You do not need to know where you will end up. You can enjoy the process by enjoying today.

As you read through my story, I want you to reflect on your own life. Do any stories resonate with you? Do any of the lessons I learned help you? Can they be applied to your life, to your current reality? To encourage reflection, I'll end each chapter with journal prompts and takeaways. Let's begin.

SECTION 1

BEING ROOTED IN YOURSELF

Maternity leave gave me opportunities to stop and think; however, I was trying to fill this time with the "busy" work of being a new mom. On my daily walks with my oldest asleep in the stroller, I would have time alone but distracted myself thinking about the future instead of enjoying the day I had. It was the most time I spent with myself, but I could not give myself my undivided attention. It was hard at times because I lived that first maternity leave with more empty cup days than full days. I didn't know I was in control of my own joy and satisfaction in life. That I was in control of the narrative. I thought someone else would do it for me. That the world owed me that one thing.

I had just given birth, and I needed to care for myself as well. But how? I didn't know how to take care of myself before the baby. Before becoming a mom, I worked long hours, didn't take care of my body, and did not respect a good night's sleep. *How could I now learn that with a child?*

I remember sitting in a sitz bath with engorged breasts and a spiking fever. My nipples were bleeding, and I could not figure it out. *How was I supposed to recover and still give to myself?* Every time he cried, my body would tense up because my raw nipples could not handle it. I ended up in emergency during that first month with a fever I developed along the way. My husband, baby, and I were all sitting in the waiting room. I was uncomfortable sitting in the unknown, in the newness, and in the unexpected. *Wasn't I supposed to be able to plan it all?*

That first year with a baby taught me to sit in the uncomfortable, in the unknown. Be able to sit alone in my own present situation. I was exhausted and constantly putting pressure on myself. I was in the mindset of highlighting everything I didn't do instead of everything I did do. Prior to becoming a mom, I would have defined myself as an optimist. I could not find optimism in that first year because I was not living in my new reality. I was trying to falsify it. During night feeds, I had a hard time sitting in my own silence. The self-doubt and negative self-talk was exhausting.

The lessons started early after giving birth. In the first couple of weeks, I had irregular or even nonexistent bowel movements. I went on a walk with my husband and newborn. I had delivered a week earlier.

It was a Saturday; after the walk, we were going to have company. It was a cold fall day in a residential area. Halfway through the walk, I had to go to the bathroom immediately and my recovering body could not hold it in very well. It took us ten minutes to get back to the lobby of our condo, and once I was in the elevator, I couldn't wait any longer. I managed to make it inside our condo, but I couldn't make it to the bathroom. Needless to say, I was humbled at that moment. That's what motherhood does to you—it humbles you.

I've been continuously humbled, and because of that, I now lead with more compassion. Feeling vulnerable and seeing everything is not about control. I was humbled through moments where control was not mine. I now make space to understand people because I take time to understand myself. My family members would tell me "you are nicer to others than to us." I finally started to realize what they meant. I have not "achieved" it yet, but it is turning into a beautiful journey. I see it in the small things. My self-talk had to improve for everything else to follow suit. When I first started waking up in the morning and meditating, the ability to spend time with myself started opening me up. I started hearing that inner voice and began internal listening on a regular basis.

I had to tune in to "who I am." I awakened myself through maternity leaves. Seeing the world with these fresh eyes by having my son, I wanted to create more positive energy for him. I needed to start with myself. Sometimes the harshest and most honest truth is the one you give yourself!

In this authentic journey of motherhood, womanhood, and being-hood, I have seen how I want to define and keep exploring myself. I found myself and now know that there is so much more that I can offer. I have found my inner authentic self. I follow my heart, my intuition, and trust this exploration. Along the way, I had another mat leave and another son. The change I felt from my first mat leave to my second one was significant. I saw a difference in my attitude. I knew what I wanted, gave myself space, asked for help, and released my expectations. I was able to enjoy even the smallest milestones. I felt happier in myself and by myself!

One important step I took to feel that true happiness was to carve out a space for myself. I created a customized sacred space in my bedroom with items that spiritually connected me, that supported the flow of creativity. I have started making areas for myself in my own home to stay calm and be with myself. The spaces don't need to be elaborate, but they do need to be intentional so they are my prompts to focus on myself. I have created quiet in my mind. Immediately when I sit down on my rug at the foot of my bed, I feel grounded. This patterned blush rug brings me closer to myself. I finally know what I want, and it is aligned with me. There will always be more, but most importantly, it is enough. I sometimes sit there for hours thinking, feeling, and writing. I make time to sit with myself.

Who am I? I am me first. I cannot be anyone else. I can be everything and nothing because I *am*. I now look at life from a lens of opportunity, gratitude, and presence. And because of this outlook, I wake up more present. I know I only get today, and I feel that in the choices I make throughout the day. I am not saying every day is perfect, but I am saying I can find the good and beauty of every day. I live from a place where I enjoy the new Monday that I get offered every week; I am grateful. It brings out creativity in me. I feel excited. When working before having kids, I used to live a life where Mondays were not this positive. That was a point in my life when I didn't comprehend that I got to choose the meaning of Mondays. From my perspective at that point, my life had become mundane, the same experiences on repeat. So here I am now, living my life, discovering what it means to be me. Discovering what I want because I get the gift of living one more day and that has meaning.

Like a tree, root yourself. That is the way you will know the deep down you, by truly being you. You have so much to offer once you are grounded in yourself. By developing your roots, your calm, no matter what weather comes your way, it will not blow you down. When you are rooted in yourself, you know who you are. No one can tell you otherwise.

It's time to open your journal and reflect on these three questions as you begin rooting yourself:

1. What brings you joy?
2. What is your purpose, beyond any role?
3. What does your voice sound like?

As this book unravels, take the time to keep pondering these questions and journaling your thoughts. We can take the time to explore ideas that are bigger than ourselves by writing about them. Everything does not make sense at once, but repetitively writing about those thoughts helps us explore what we want.

Writing also moves it from an idea to a form. When we write it down, it starts to become real and is no longer just a concept in our head. The idea can get out of your head and become a reality.

Somewhere you will find the calm and truth of who you are. Pause, reflect, and take the time to uncover.

THE ROOTED TREE

When we watch movies, the tree has wisdom
Advice
Peace
A message, a connection.
In my visions, these rooted trees
Once had more branches, now they have more leaves.
I am now a part of the forest
Part of the landscape, part of the greenery
Always carrying a message to move forward and lead from
the heart.
Trusting and releasing expectations.
Listening to the wisdom of the wind.
Feel the elements: the rain, the snow, the sun
Never alone, always a part of the bigger picture of the forest
A part of the story, a part of the journey.
The forest grows in me
And I grow to be a part of the forest.

WHAT BRINGS YOU JOY?

When I am on the right path or in the right place, I keep seeing an image of a deep rooted tree in my visualizations or in real life. For instance, it shows up on shoes, on a piece of paper, on paintings—absolutely anywhere. I am the deep rooted tree with the branches reaching high. I am present and intentional so now I see the trees as the Universe's message. On a trip to Poland, I spoke to intuitive women in our family and learned about the intuitive women of the past. My paternal great-grandmother kept finding religious pendants and crosses in nature as her sign. We all get these intuitive signs and hits, we just have to listen and see them. Take note of yours. What symbols or messages come to you? Are you taking the time to notice?

Now when I close my eyes, I see trees, and I become this tree rooted in the Earth. I feel a stability running through me, unlike ever before. I finally stand on my own two feet. When I walk into a new opportunity or decision, I feel the love and support of my female ancestors supporting me and my big ideas. They support the feminine energy I am exploring. They themselves lived in the masculine energy. As I write this section of the book tonight, I am listening to healing Gregorian chanting, and I see myself transform from woman to horse to a horse with wings. I feel free. These are all thoughts and experiences I did not make space for before. Now, as I sit in the sacred space I have created in my bedroom, I know I am exactly where I am supposed to be. I know how I want to take up space! I had this freedom I was chasing and now I found it. It was here the whole time. I am in the energy of flow, passion, and fullness.

During my second mat leave, I was seeing a naturopath in our local community. There was another practitioner offering energy sessions. Prior to this, I had never worked with a practitioner in this way. It didn't fully make sense to me, but I was intrigued. I knew I was interested and ready to add in the offerings that could come my way. I was ready to receive. I went for multiple hypnotherapy sessions and began learning about the power of the feminine and masculine energy. Regardless of gender, we all have these energies within. The Yin and Yang. The Sun and Moon. In our North American workplaces, we tend to be in the masculine energy, in the doing, not in the receiving. With the pandemic and spending more time with ourselves at home, as a community, we have connected to the feminine energy of creativity, receiving, and nurturing. As we allow this receiving as a community, abundance will keep coming in. We are now happy to connect with it. We do not understand what it all means, but we do know this is for us!

Family picnicking is something that we took up during the pandemic, in the middle of my second mat leave. It put a smile on my face. We would stop and have a picnic somewhere convenient. As if we were traveling in Europe and enjoying the local parks. We learned about beautiful green spaces near our house. Prior to having children, my husband and I visited Venice with some friends. We purchased lunch: a fresh baguette and some delicious cheeses and meats from the grocery store and sat along the canals with our friends to look at the gondolas. It was memorable. I felt a strong connection of eating outside and being present to where we were. We were aware of the scents, the sounds, and the visual stimulation. Picnicking shows you how to be present in the moment.

As a family during the pandemic, we biked to our local bakery, purchased some pizza buns and doughnuts, then stopped along a path, surrounded by luscious trees. It had been here for years, but this was the first time we truly took the time to enjoy it. We sat on our waterproof blanket and ate lunch as a family. Many people walked by us that day and some took a moment to pause their walk to say,

"Beautiful picnic." I thought to myself that it was simple to bring joy, not only to ourselves, but to those walking by us. That's how simple it is to share joy with your children, with your spouse, with yourself. And being open to the joy of even small acts in life can pour happiness into others by witnessing the beauty.

In the same week, we were having dinner at my in-laws, a regular Sunday activity at their house. First, we had homemade chicken noodle soup. Then we had delicious chicken cutlets and salmon filets with fresh cucumbers and potatoes from their garden. After dinner we went outside to the yard to see their new kittens. We all sat on the grass and talked. My in-laws, boys, husband, and brother-in-law. At that moment, I felt grateful to sit with all of them in this one place. They had lived in this house for eight years, but this was the first time we sat on their grass. Similar to the Venice experience, it was memorable! My boys were picking corn, cucumbers, and tomatoes from their garden and sitting back down to munch on what they collected. We started talking about animals and my in-laws' upbringing on their family farms. Their love for animals had really shaped them into who they are today and how they view their connection to nature. It was a conversation we've never had before we sat and had that impromptu picnic.

The moment of pause and appreciation warmed me from the inside. It was joy. It wasn't because we were in another country or in a new home. It was right now, in the moment. It happened with our current jobs, with our current pay, in our normal routine. It was uneventful and it was meaningful. That fullness—that true life satisfaction—was there all along.

When you sit in the quiet and appreciate it, that is where joy lives. The joy that is yours and that just you can feel. We have to pause to hear it and feel it.

I remember when a friend came over and I was giving her a tour of our house. She said, "You live in a beautiful area!"

Before that moment, I was living in our townhouse dreaming about moving into a larger, detached house. But after she said that, it clicked. **I need to be where I am. I need to enjoy it and have gratitude.** That's exactly what I did from that moment on. I moved the furniture around on the balcony and in our backyard; we could now use it intentionally. I purposefully designated space for kids and outdoor eating. I stopped waiting for the next house. She was right. Love where you are! I now use the home because we get to live here today.

What a gift it is to have this home and be surrounded by nature while living five minutes away from my parents. We have great bike paths around us. We regularly stop to watch the blue jays and cardinals. There is a home down the street that has a bird feeder in their backyard, and we cannot help but stop and watch these colorful creatures fly in to eat. Sometimes the squirrels come and grab some for themselves. It looks like an obstacle course for them; their weight is too much for the feeder.

My 5-year-old shared that he was sad that the birds were migrating. He started to cry and my husband had to leave earlier to the bus to help him calm down. It is crucial to notice when things change and appreciate them when they are here. Just like with the house, I need to remind myself to love what I am, what I have, and what I offer right now. I am the best version of myself, and I am thankful! Just like with the birds, I also need to realize that change is inevitable. Appreciate what is NOW.

FULLNESS

Life's fullness—what is that?
It is not attached to a bank account
Not a career change or promotion
Not one more child
Not a new house
It is the beauty in the small, in the minute.
The scent of your hand soap
A perfect curl in your hair
The sunrise right when you wake up
The movement of leaves on a tree
Family garbage truck watching
Gluing crafts into shapes
Warm laundry
Clean lemony fresh dishes
The Saturday morning sleep-in
The soft teddy you put in their bed
Your kiss goodnight as they fall asleep.
The fullness of life lives in those everyday moments.

Before having kids, in my early twenties, I applied for my master's program. I had three options of programs. I got accepted to each one and now had to choose. I called one of my friends to help with the decision. She knew about all the programs so I thought she'd give the best advice. Her life advice still sticks in my brain: "They're all champagne choices." All were good options. When you only have good options, you cannot make a bad decision. There is no wrong choice. Viewing your options in that way helps you alleviate negative worries and focus on the positive.

As the year was coming to an end, I was thinking about these champagne choices. Remembering, all good options. Over all these years this quote continuously rings true. With the last few days of the year, as a family, we started working on our Year Compass. It is a booklet translated into different languages that helps you close out the previous year and plan the new one. It's a way of prioritizing what you want by reflecting on your past and getting excited about your future. It has questions for you to answer, and the better the responses, the more you will learn about yourself and your year. It uncovers repeat behaviors so you are in control of the new year and there is always something to be grateful for.

I suggest you visit https://yearcompass.com to get this booklet, especially when you start the new year. Take a moment to celebrate successes no matter how small. Notice what you liked and didn't like, and see the significance of 365 days. This ensures that when you move into the next year, you will know what to make space for and what you want to receive from it.

It was really effective the previous year, so we decided to do our sibling gift exchange and the Year Compass for New Year's Eve. We put the kids to sleep and reflected on our past year. It was a pivotal moment in our family as we shared from this place of continuous exploration. We now share the real version of ourselves. We can't help but be there for each other and want to share from that place.

Having regular moments to reflect on the champagne choices in your life is vital to staying present and grateful. The beginning of the year is a great opportunity because with a clean slate you can start with breaking your year into quarters and further into months. The quarters build the progress of the year, and the months let you soak in each of those quarters so you can get even closer to the goals you set.

There are two other parts of the year that are natural launch times: the beginning of spring and the new school year in September. Take these moments to pause and see what you want to keep moving into the rest of the year. Use this time with purpose to launch your big ideas and soak up the good ones. Also, the beginning of July is the beginning of the second half of the year. This is a time for self-reflection. With every passing month, take a pause to write down your learnings from the month. When you treat your year with respect, you start noticing more details about it, and it doesn't just go by. You live it with purpose. You create a fuller year when you are intentional about soaking it in.

$*\ *\ *$

One of my favorite activities is taking walks. One day when my oldest was around seven months, we went to the local park. I had gone to that park many times before, but this time was different. We sat on a bench, as we always did, and I noticed the details: how the ducks swam, the birds chirped, and the leaves blew in the wind. It was memorable yet no different from the day before. I couldn't believe that I had missed this before. Walks are refreshing and get me to a place of joy. Walking to school, to the park, to my parents. It is amazing to be outdoors. I even enjoy walking in different weather and temperatures, rain or shine or snow—although I draw the line at thunder. It is lovely appreciating Canada's four seasons.

"THE GREATEST GIFT YOU CAN GIVE YOUR FAMILY IS YOUR HAPPINESS."

–Hina Khan

My sister and her family came over one Sunday for brunch. At some point in the day, she started having a headache. She kept telling me how much her head hurt. I heard it, but it kept rolling right off of me. I did not engage with the topic. She kept saying it until she realized she was not going to get any additional complaining time. I was able to protect myself from her negative commentary. This freed her from the negative state to accept the headache by not giving her headache anymore stage time. She later went on a run and immediately felt the joy come back. It is not about judging, it is about not giving the wrong things in your life stage time. **You want to be a part of conversations that keep adding to your life. Leave the conversations that are not serving you.**

Reflecting on mindset, I regularly tell her that life is a series of fortunate and unfortunate events—you get to choose the narrative. Positive and negative things happen every day, but you attach an emotion to it. It can just stay neutral once you accept the reality. The next day after her headache, she called me in the morning. She listed all the positive things today, including that her baby slept for twenty minutes of her thirty-minute yoga class. She decided to appreciate the day and go for a walk outside. Later, her windshield wipers and the wiper fluid weren't working properly. Instead of getting frustrated, after some reflection she felt, "Well, this was a learning experience."

She called me after all of this to share that I showed her the importance of not dwelling on the negative parts of the day and enjoying the day from a place of gratitude. The key is to accept the reality of today. It just is.

> "YOU HAVE ONE WILD AND PRECIOUS LIFE— JUST ONE. ONE OPPORTUNITY TO LIVE THAT LIFE IN YOUR OWN WAY. ONE CHANCE TO LIVE THROUGH EACH STAGE OF YOUR LIFE, AND WITH NO CHANCE TO REHEARSE, SO YOU WANT TO MAKE THAT LIFE COUNT."
>
> **—Maureen Gaffney**

One day after I committed to writing this book, I was making a savannah diorama with my son. As we were creating it, he said, "This is going to be big, bold, and beautiful."

Big, bold, and beautiful. I smiled. That is exactly what I want, not just for the diorama, but for my life. I am living a big, bold, and beautiful life. Let me take up space in my own life. Find the BOLDNESS from within!

Over the last couple of weeks, playfulness is a word that keeps showing up for me. Observing my kids during the pandemic, I saw how playful children are. How they can find the fun in everything: jumping on a couch, building Lego to be a rocket or a car, gardening, eating herbs, or playing farmer at home on a random Thursday. They find that true joy. The type of joy that brings happiness to your whole body. The type of joy that makes you comfortable being bold. It's inspiring.

When I watercolor, talk with inspiring people, go to the park with my boys, watch the sunrise, journal in the evening, learn a new sport, or improve my catching, I start to experience that same full-body joy. That feeling that makes you smile from ear to ear. I am now playful and want that in everything that I do. Starting my coaching business with a great social media and website team helped me launch my business in a playful way (nataliaharhaj.com). Yes, I was working on content and my yearly plan, but in the meantime, I was enjoying writing and creating my offerings and my experiences. **Playfulness needs to exist in your everyday life to build the bold.**

It was instrumental to my personal discovery when I took

the time to break my year into quarters with a purpose: Discovery, Abundance, Implementation, and Level Up. Let's start at the beginning. As I was going through my mat leave, I knew I was missing another piece to my professional development. I felt like I was missing something. I met a coach who shared the potential growth, which got me thinking about my life success, not as a role improvement at work but by highlighting the feelings that I wanted to see regularly in my life. I drew out a diagram and knew what was meaningful. By the time the next year rolled around, I was ready. I knew the feelings I wanted to feel in my year, in my life.

For the first time as a family, we set goals in the new year. In that process, I broke the year into quarters: Discovery, Abundance, Implementation, and Level Up. These were words I selected to reflect the year I wanted to experience. I kept true to the motto and felt the growth in my weeks immediately. I was living with a purpose. I got that to seep into my week, month, and year. I knew why I was doing this and that I wanted to see more in myself. All the offerings for me came into my life with regular momentum and peaceful thought. I was being purposeful with my life. With every month, I reached more and more into the quarterly goal. By the time three months finished, it was achieved to a feeling of fullness. It was not about accomplishment but leaving enough space and intention to uncover more. To dig deeper into myself. This is how I set it out for myself:

Quarter 1: Discovery	Quarter 2: Abundance
• Uncover the unknown within yourself and the environment	• Fullness for all parts of you
Quarter 3: Implementation	Quarter 4: Level Up
• Activate everything you see for yourself	• There is more, so much more!

I put the goals for the quarters and the feelings for the year on my bathroom mirror, and I got started. This was the starting point for me, and it could be for you too. What do you want from your year? What feeling are you seeking? Is it courage or to radiate? To be bold, mindful, soulful, spontaneous, or creative? Whatever it is, make sure you label it. As the year unfolds, you will be conscious of moments that make you feel better and more. Make space for yourself in your week, month, year. You will see life experiences through a different lens. A day will have more to offer than before when you live from a place of purpose.

There are moments that will—and do—define your year, and this process did that for me. What are the moments that define it for you? The Universe shows me where I am supposed to be through intuition and signs. My responsibility is to be present to the events that happen to me and around me and to feel emotionally full. I feel like anything that is happening to me fills my heart with emotions. Writing seems to be an effective way to pour it out and examine what I've got.

As December ended, my husband and I kept laughing that it was about to be his year because he started new programs and had bigger goals. He signed up to work with a personal development coach, bought new running gear in preparation for all-season runs, including marathons, and bought a new road bike. It kept coming. We were driving to my in-laws on New Year's Day for my father-in-law's birthday and we started discussing his running group, which includes my brothers-in-law and brother. We stated: "Our family is going to have to run, it will be a part of our regular activities." As we were driving to their neighborhood we understood why everyone would be starting or increasing their running goals. It was all part of the community's success. The next day he was on Strava creating a group goal where everyone commits to an amount, and there is a communal goal we want to achieve by the end of the year. Everyone commits a yearly distance, but together we achieve the goal. Now I know what my husband's year meant: he was the metronome. He is keeping the pace for our family this year.

In the morning, my kids woke up, and my husband took them downstairs. I went back to bed for an hour. I had not been having dreams, but it came to me then. The frame of my glasses broke in my dream, down the nose bridge. I no longer needed my glasses because I could see, I had knowledge. It came to me out of the blue. I awoke on day two of the year knowing we were already off to a dynamic start. In the background, downstairs, my youngest kept having deep belly laughs, ones filled with joy. I felt instantly that it was a great year and it had just started.

* * *

Who am I without my labels? As we began a new year, I was reflecting
on how there is so much more for me to offer to myself and to others.
I am more than all those labels I hold onto: daughter, wife, mother,
employee, owner, artist, writer, etc. I am so much more. That is why
I do the work. I can see more breaking open in me. There is beauty
in that abundant me. I just *am.* I already am all of these things and
none of these at the same time. I do not have to achieve them, and at
the same time, I can be all of these things. I simply *am.*

I have a necklace that I use to ask questions and see what comes—it's
my pendulum. It helps me better understand all the intuitive meanings
to clarify what is around the corner. Even though my intuition already
told me the answers, I ask the pendulum to confirm my knowing. This
has turned into a calming grounding activity, specifically when the
boys go to sleep.

1. Grounding question: Do I have pineapple at home? *YES. (We
    had bought one on the weekend.)*
2. Do I start this mastermind now? *YES.*
3. Is it going to be one and a half hours? *YES.*
4. Is it going to be two hours? *YES. (Okay?! It means that I will
    have a group session for one and a half hours and a thirty-
    minute breakout session between two people.)*

5. Are twenty-four people going to register? *YES. (Twenty-four did not formally register into the group program, but a lot of people reached out and asked questions. And more individuals engaged after the launch of the workshop.)*

I'd asked many questions over the last six months. *Do I go to this event? Should I pay for this? Do I turn left? Should I pack a lunch?* And the list goes on. **I am a woman who is intuitively being pulled in a direction and these nudges keep me going down a beautiful path**. I stopped making my choices because I know intuition will bring it to my attention when required. The path will present itself, and I have to listen to the nudge. *Is it a pull toward or a push away?*

I now understand who I am, when to go, and when to stop. The pendulum is a calming activity that I do to ground myself because in truth I already know the answer from my intuition.

In the past, I saw maternity leave as running hurdles that slowed down my growth, especially for my career. I created a lot during this time. It was an influential moment of time for creation. A time to dream, want, reflect, and contemplate. I asked myself *what do I want my life to be like? What feelings do I want to have in my life?* In those days of breastfeeding, with vomit on my clothing and days' old dirty hair, I wanted to have a long and successful career, like Hazel McCallion, nicknamed "Hurricane Hazel" because of her sheer strength, who worked well into her nineties. By stating that, I took the pressure off of myself to be successful in the next couple of years. I gave myself until 101. That idea gave me the space I needed to decide on the life I wanted in the next ten years, not just in my career.

Why was I even here? What did I want to do with my one beautiful life? How do I continue to create from a place of joy? How do I radiate my best self every day by filling my cup first? At my own pace and with my own ideas of success. I was not about to chase anything or everything. I was respecting the time I got to exist and be here. I knew the answers would come when I was ready to receive them. In truth, I used my mat leave as the springboard to speed up the answer to the question: *What do I want out of my life?* Even when I asked that question, however, I knew the answer was already inside of me.

PLANT YOUR SEEDS

1. Label and write down the five emotions and feelings you want. Put the list in a visible spot so you can go back to it and see it every day (I put mine on my bathroom mirror).

    _____

    _____

    _____

    _____

    _____

2. When you live a day from the place of these feelings, what does the year, quarter, month, week, day look like for you?

    _____

    _____

    _____

3. Find activities that ground you. An activity that when you're engaged in it, everything else washes away. For instance, running, walking, meditating, waking up earlier than others in your household, or lighting a candle. What activities ground you?

    _____

    _____

    _____

    _____

4. Keep track of the days and weeks when you learned or experienced something new from a different emotion. For instance, did you start waking up earlier? Do you now have a different morning routine and are more present starting the day? Take note of it. This is where you will start to see the goodness of everything you are doing.

_____

_____

_____

_____

_____

_____

5. Describe your true self.

_____

_____

_____

_____

_____

_____

_____

_____

_____

_____

I ALREADY AM

I already am, who I want to be
I am all those things I aspire to be because in all of this I am me.
In this journey, I will find my voice because it is in me
I will begin to take up space
Boundaryless.

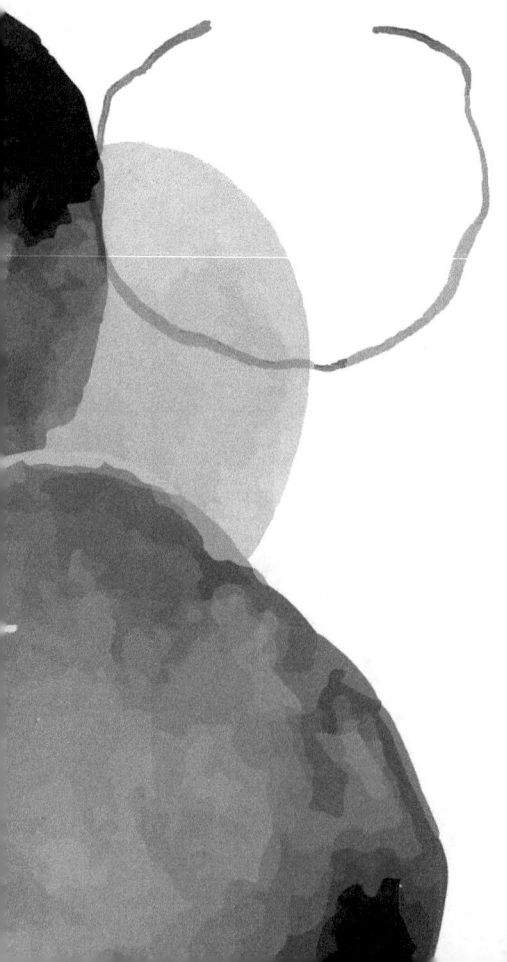

WHAT IS YOUR PURPOSE?

I woke up early one morning with the memory of us on the day we left the hospital after my oldest was born. I remember getting him dressed and ready to go in his cozy red onesie. It was a balmy day in November, and I felt the warmth of the sun that day. My husband went to get the car while I was waiting with my mama in the lobby. Suddenly I burst into tears. They were pouring out. It was a few things: the hormones, the changes, seeing our new baby, taking him home. I felt the significance of that moment, and I still do even today when I reflect on it. That was the first step in our journey as a family, as parents, as new versions of ourselves. Thinking back, this was a moment where my reality changed forever, in a life-altering way. It was a monumental day that led to my growth as a human being. A day filled with opportunity and the importance of it. I was overwhelmed with gratitude that my mom and husband were there to get us into the car for us to begin our sunny drive home.

After that it was not all clear skies—it was challenging, and not everything was going as I initially thought. I had many expectations of myself, my spouse, our new baby, our life. The earlier version of me lived in a victim mentality. I did not fully embrace the life I got gifted each day. After the self-work, discovery, and release to my true self, **I realized the power of today. Tomorrow is irrelevant if I do not enjoy today**. Where I am right now. What I get to experience. But not at that moment, none of that was coming in for me because I wasn't letting it in. It was not yet part of my reality. I didn't understand that I had the ability to change my life's perspective.

Until becoming a mom, I had no idea that this exhaustion was different from anything else I had experienced. The type of exhaustion that makes your brain foggy for weeks, even months. Feeling so tired that you feel detached from yourself, unfamiliar with who you even are. The one that makes your hours long but your months disappear. The kind that makes you forget a world outside of your bedroom or your home, yet makes you crave it. The one that makes you look at your home and not understand how something could look so disorganized. The kind that makes you unfamiliar with what you did a minute ago, let alone an hour ago. Mundane questions swirled in my mind: *When did I last wash my hair? Or do laundry? Buy groceries? Vacuum? Or nap?*

My first time around, there was fear in everything I did, and I remember being a martyr in a lot of those moments. I created conflict in my home because I had conflict in myself. No one could help me as I did not know how to help myself. I often thought about the everyday challenges, the loneliness, the exhaustion. My self-talk was not about overcoming it or enjoying it. My self-talk kept me sitting and staying in the hard. I didn't know I was already in the easy. I was already my future self, I just had to choose it. I wanted to complain, so I complained often, usually to my husband or my sister. I stayed in this unsatisfied, unfulfilled place, which took a toll on me, my joy, and my relationships.

But with my second mat leave, I was different. I had a better under-standing of who I was and what I wanted; even in those moments when I could not control the outcome, I released the worry, the stress. I was a couple of months into being a mama of two and remember waking up early to breastfeed my baby. I felt gratitude and absolute happiness as I watched the sunrise with its bright oranges and pinks. I was happy and so was the sun. I woke up differently than I did with my first; I woke up with gratitude. I made these moments special, and I celebrated them with joy attached. Yes, it was exhausting, and at the same time, I could still feel joy.

What I came to learn in this process of motherhood was to take time for myself. To grab a hot coffee, leave the house, go for a walk. To brush my teeth with calm instead of rushing. To sit on the balcony reading a book or take a nap while the baby was sleeping. **When the narrative in your head is negative, it's important to change it.** Eventually, I started appreciating the silence and would sit and enjoy the stillness.

Regardless of what's happening in your life, you need to take time for yourself. Some days you'll have an hour; some days it might only be five minutes. In the end, be purposeful with the time that you have. Only you know what you need to fill your cup. Everyone around you will feel when your cup is full. Most importantly, you will know when it is full. You will start filling your cup in the moments of chaos and loudness. **You will start seeing that today is a gift that doesn't come again. Today is only today.**

When your kids are playing and pulling toys from each other, instead of focusing on the screaming, you'll focus on the beauty of siblinghood. Instead of seeing the task of diaper changes, you'll see the beauty of alone time and seeing their growth. Instead of seeing the spills, you'll see their ability to clean it up. **Life is a work in progress. It is not about being perfect but taking a moment to change the self-talk in your head.**

SIBLINGHOOD

The love, to a brother, to a sister
Has fullness, has light.
Your soul smiles when they walk into the room
They give you a constant, they walk at your pace even when
they are running.
Their arms embrace like no other
The playfulness, the learning, the imagination
You feel you can conquer it all
You have a bond that binds forever.
Let it be.
It's the laughter that fills when you are in their space
When you are in their bubble
No one can step in
No one can change the moment
For the person standing by
Joy, compassion, immeasurable love is all they can see.

We were having some renovations at home and my full-length mirror ended up in my bathroom in front of the toilet. I was getting ready for bed one night and as I was looking at myself, there was something fascinating about the changing woman's body. Between breastfeeding and getting older, your breasts have this wisdom to them. My wise breasts. There's something lovely in that, especially when you embrace it. When you embrace the fact that this is the body that has given, created, and provided. Then it just is. You simply acknowledge this is what it looks like. I've had these moments of looking at my body as it's changing. My physical body and my mind have changed a lot in this experience of motherhood. I understand that the changes can make us uncomfortable. Our bodies are no longer oblivious to what they can create and nurture. My body has lived. I embrace these new breasts for their realness! Maybe in the end, I have changed a lot and my breasts show it the best. I've lived. My body has shown my trans-formation—it shows my *beinghood*.

We often think that when we become a mama, we become someone new. "Ooh, look at the new you; you look great as a mama; this really suits you." But you are not new, you have been in there the whole time. That *new* person is really the deep down YOU. She has emerged, and she has a presence. Give her the space she needs to flourish, to release it all. Beauty radiates when we dig a bit deeper. I felt like I finally met myself. I started advocating for myself out of love. I did what was best for me and my family. It was then that I could explore what I really wanted out of my life, my work, my days, weeks, and years.

It is like a flower when the petals fall away, who are you at the core without the layers protecting you? Who is the deep down you? Emerge. Emerge that being from the depths of you. Do it for yourself, and everyone around you will benefit from being in your presence. You are a gift, and when you accept that, you will start growing and flourishing. You are not a flower but a whole garden, a whole forest. You were there the entire time.

MY AFFIRMATIONS

I am present, I appreciate the moments I am presented
I let myself be.
People are inspired when they talk to me, they enjoy sharing
their wins
People like to work with me and invest in themselves through
me.
When talking with me, we both reach our fullest potential
because we support unraveling growth.
I feel abundant and filled with opportunity
Great things come our way
The Universe connects me to the right people at the right time.
I trust my intuitive hits
An idea comes to me and I act on it from this place of trust
and positivity.
I do not focus on the HOW, I let it be and it comes with ease
I know who I am and my place in the world
I am a creator of multigenerational projects
I am playful, spontaneous, and do things from a place of joy.
I am the person I always knew I was
This will only grow from here
I invest in myself and my ideas.
I am a person who creates and opportunities come to me
I have found myself and I love who I am deep down
Who I am at the core.

I took time for myself on Sunday and went biking at a leisurely pace. I was loving where I got to be and that I got to do this alone. I felt the joy of biking in my quiet thoughts of gratitude along a forested path close to home. Complete calm. A group of bikers went past me on their regular group bike ride. They swarmed me, then went right past me. It looked like I was riding a tricycle behind my older siblings and their friends. At that moment, I smiled. *Part of being is enjoying where you are.* I thought to myself, I do not want to bike in that way. I liked my pace and my reason for biking. It wasn't out of a fear or lacking belief in my ability but finally accepting what I wanted at that moment. I wanted to be an occasional recreational bike rider and enjoy my five kilometers alone or with family. I was finally able to say exactly what I wanted and would not be pushed or pulled by someone else's intentions. I was rooted in me, in my truth. I know that I am. Release all expectations—especially yours—and be rooted in yourself!

Paid support is consistent support. Over the course of the last few years, the people who I paid were the ones who had set meetings with me, checked-in consistently, made sure I was moving forward, and consistently took care of my children. They made sure that whatever we worked on was moving in the right direction. This is how I figured out what I wanted to do and how I wanted to spend my time. I released my expectations that I had to do it alone, without consistent support.

I can make what I am making and still find a way to help myself by knowing what I want. Solutions come to me regularly but not always as I anticipated. It comes as the Universe thinks best for me.

In my mind, I keep envisioning a third mat leave: I will continue paying for additional support for myself, my family, and our home. This is a mat leave that does not exist but is vivid in my mind. I can see that the support is game changing to my recovery and to my growth as a human being. I am able to focus on getting better and slowing down at the same time. Pause instead of go. I will not overextend myself. I won't rush to do laundry and cleaning. I will make time for myself and what my body needs. I now have the words to ask for what I need because I did the self-work to identify it. I know what I want and I smile. I fill my cup first.

MOMMY GUILT

I have to be there for my husband, my partner
For my children
Now, I realized that the best
Is to be there for me.
The rest will follow
And I will be more than I could have imagined
I will bring a new energy to everything I do.
You can only fill when you are full
You will know the feeling when you reach it
It will be a sense of overflow
Everyone's cups will fill from your excess.

My brother-in-law recently stated: "Now when you walk into a room, it is different. You used to be in the negative and create conflict. Now you leave us with big ideas and positivity."

He is right. Before, we would have Sunday dinners with the family and I would have discussions about politics, social justice, any topic that came up that week in the news. Not from a place of change but from a place of worry and venting. It was not productive. Hina Khan states: **"Leave people with a sense of increase."** That is something I am now practicing in my life. Coming to situations with abundance and encouragement instead of the comments I had before. My previous words were wrapped up in my fears and internal conflict. **I now show people the fullness of life because I make time to feel it.** It feels kinder, and it is easier to find joy.

My friends have shared that if someone wants to make more money or manifest a business, they should call me. This is exactly the type of conversations I've enjoyed having with people. People have started sharing their big wants with me. Now when I go to a gathering, people come to me for exactly these conversations. I even share my intuitive hits and add to their big dreams. For some people, during these conversations, I can see what is possible, it just hasn't taken form yet. I truly believe the wants are there to be achieved, and we must believe they're ours for the taking. In this one beautiful life, we do not have time to listen to that negative small voice inside. That is the voice we need to ignore until it becomes insignificant or disappears behind our large voice of intuition.

* * *

On Instagram, I had posted about becoming a writer and publishing the next year. The outpouring of support was wonderful! People wished me well and sent their kind words. I created a "hype squad" Excel list for myself to note how many people wanted me to strive, accomplish, and excel. I now feel like they are with me with every new project I take on. My group keeps growing, and I feel supported by this invisible community of people. Social media is not all bad. It can leave you with this sense of community, a group that you wouldn't otherwise put together. Create your own hype squad list! There may be more people on it than you think. Make sure to put your name first on the list.

ADVICE TO MY PAST SELF

Do something in life that makes you enjoy Mondays
Brings out your creativity and excitement.
Long hours at a desk will not get you to where you want
Trust in yourself, trust in the process
Release control, release it, and let go of the outcome
Find work you want to do
That you get to do,
Work you want to contribute to.
When you work from the heart, you truly add value
You bring growth to the industry, yourself, and your peers.
A salary is not tied to joy
Money is energy, make it and spend it with love
In a way that moves you
Share the wealth.
Your kids will see this
They mirror it back to you.
Don't run away, lean forward
Be intrigued
Enjoy the moment, not where it is leading to
Don't be so serious; play and enjoy
Slow down, even stop!
Let it go, it will come with EASE.
Release control
Do activities in silence. Be alone with your thoughts
You cannot be everything to everyone, not even to your kids
or your spouse.
Listen in those little moments, during the everyday tasks
To your thoughts, to your intuition
You do not have to do anything
You get to pick.

Accept compliments because you are a gift to the world, to
your community
To your family
Accept feedback from the right people.
Everyone does not get an opinion on your life
It just doesn't matter.
You choose and choose for you
Everyone will benefit, especially you
You will change the environment around yourself and radiate
this beingness.

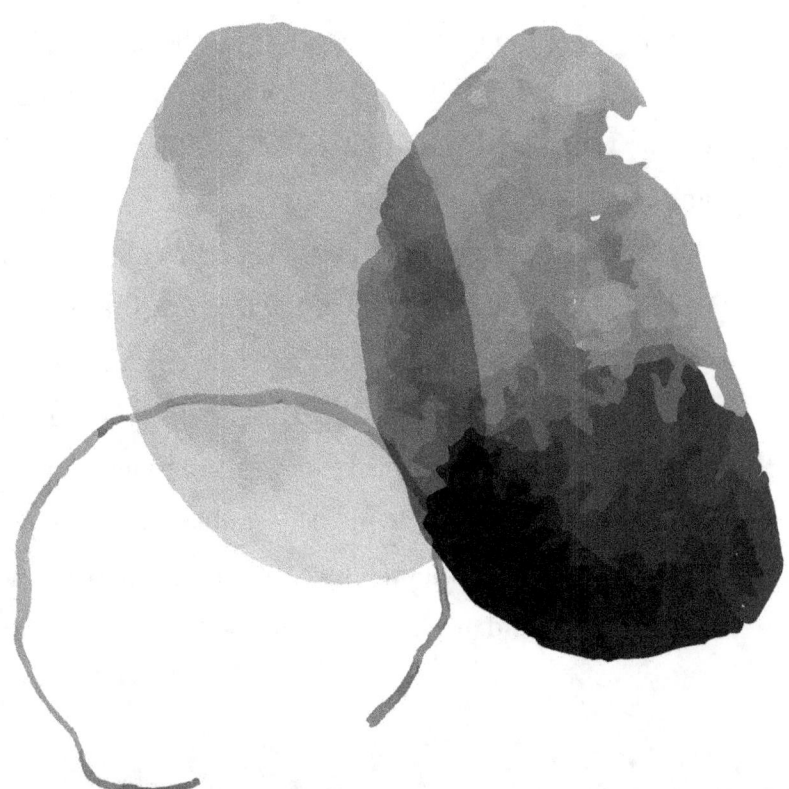

Mama bear. It's the feeling that comes out of you when you have a baby. I never felt this emotion before having my first. It was bigger than me and stronger. It came out when people were not doing the "right" thing with him and weren't providing the care that I thought was required. I had high expectations, and no one could ever meet them because even I couldn't meet my own expectations. I was constantly measuring myself beside an unachievable standard. It was deep in my core, and I had a hard time controlling the largeness of this feeling. It took up a lot of headspace and created a lot of internal conflict. With my second, it subsided slightly. For my well-being, I am happy it did. It was exhausting being on this high alert in every situation. Regularly seeing what I was not happy with.

Where did that mama bear feeling come from? I felt that with both of my boys. I thought maybe that it was hormones, that it wasn't the real me. Then I watched my in-law's cat, Lala; she was always aware of who was getting close to her young kittens. I saw in her demeanor and eyes how I felt after having my kids. A mother who needs space but is also trying to release motherhood. Is it innately sitting in all of us? **How can we transform that big mama bear feeling into something productive and kinder to ourselves?** How do we accept that feeling without the fear and disappointment?

During my second mat leave, I could not be everything for my oldest, nor did he want that from me. He wanted his own experiences, some with and some without me. It was about interdependence. We coexist in this family and are human beings with our own wants and needs.

Even at five, he knows what he wants. He is learning to talk about those big emotions and his desires. We all need the space to reach our internal power. We get to witness each other grow and dig deeper into who we are. I am part of my family's story, of the world's story.

"EVERYONE, WHEN THEY ARE YOUNG, KNOWS WHAT THEIR PERSONAL LEGEND IS. AT THAT POINT IN THEIR LIVES, EVERYTHING IS CLEAR AND EVERYTHING IS POSSIBLE. THEY ARE NOT AFRAID TO DREAM, AND TO YEARN FOR EVERY-THING THEY WOULD LIKE TO SEE HAPPEN TO THEM IN THEIR LIVES. BUT, AS TIME PASSES, A MYSTERIOUS FORCE BEGINS TO CONVINCE THEM THAT IT WILL BE IMPOSSIBLE FOR THEM TO REALIZE THEIR PERSONAL LEGEND."

–Paulo Coelho, *The Alchemist*

Through this journey of intuitive listening, I remember the nudges I received as a child but didn't act upon or got scared of as an adult because of the vastness instead of releasing expectations. I thought I was daydreaming and did not realize the Universe was showing me my life. By letting the Universe take me on this journey, here I am. I am available for the turns and curves, the unknowns. Again, realizing it is not about getting to a specific ending but letting the story unravel and seeing what it wants from me. Knowing when this stays with me and when this delightful gem is passed onto the next person. I am starting to see my Personal Legend again. It is similar to what I said as a child, but more things have shown themselves. I am now ready to listen and take the necessary action. I do not accept this as daydreaming, I am accepting it as my life. The task is bigger than me, but it will make more and more sense with every intuitive step that I take. I am ready!

My washroom wall is a mesmerizing place filled with goals, quotes, and to-dos. This is where I keep the items I want to keep top of mind. Here are some of the messages I have left for myself over the years:

- "If you want to go FAST, go alone. If you want to go far, go together." –African proverb
- "Go as far as you can see. When you get there, you will see how you can go further." –Thomas Carlyle
- Goals: 1. Work remotely over the summers to be with my husband and the boys; 2. Pick up the boys from school and have dinner with them; 3. Achieve financial abundance.
- Natalia, you are meant for great things!
- "You are not a drop in the ocean, you are an ocean in a drop."–Rumi

- You can only control three things: your actions, your words, the handling of your own emotions.
- Quarterly goal: right now it is on ABUNDANCE.

On the days that I spend the time to read and embody these feelings and goals, I know I am off to a good start. The bathroom wall messages remind me of the big goals, the true purpose of it all, because you can get lost in your everyday tasks. The bathroom messaging reminds me to deal with parts of my purpose today and to keep them top of mind. You move everything forward a little bit every day.

My cousin was showing me the eaves trough at their house and how there was a leak in a small section. He said: "It is not a big leak. However, the constant dripping for a long period of time onto the cement has created a hole." I needed to hear that message. It is not about making big sweeping changes immediately. Instead, it is about being consistent in the smallest actions. **Consistent small actions make a big impact.**

MAMA, WHEN WILL YOU DIE?

When it is my time, I will have to leave
It will be my turn.
I will live on in you and in the world you live
I will not look the same but you will hear me
My body will not be able to stay
But my voice and memory will be with you.
My energy will surround you when you need it most
When you seek me you will find me
It will be the support or love you need that day
It will be a soulful hug
I will be there for the everyday and the special moments.
That is why we live for today and the gratitude that it has been
gifted to us!
In today, we accept the reality that it is fleeting and it happens
only once.

Moments—when you put them all together, you have a LIFE. Treat those moments like a gift. The questions from your child, their ability to learn a new task, the way their face can change in twenty-four hours, the beauty of a hug or a kiss from a family member, moments of love and support. You don't have to chase them; they come to you. The moments land on your lap. You just have to receive them. Let them in. Release expectations and accept the moments. Pause and see them. They are right here. You are exactly where you should be. Let that knowing radiate from you. You always knew who you were. Finally, you are letting others see it too.

There are moments in your life when you realize you're juggling both plastic and glass balls, in your personal and professional life. There are moments that are nonnegotiable. They're the glass ones: a child's recital or a crucial team meeting. You get to decide what is important to you and define it as a glass ball. I am thinking back to a moment where I felt like I was holding two glass balls: one for my job and another for a friend's wedding. I had a job opportunity come up to go and travel to learn more about a client and their company. It was on the same day as a friend's wedding. A week before the wedding, this opportunity landed in my lap. I had to make that decision immediately because the rest of the team was also flying. It was a challenge because I was making the decision from a place of fear, a fear of what that would mean to my colleagues if I didn't go, how this would impact my working relationship with the client. What that would mean to my career growth if I didn't go.

I called my friend at the last minute and canceled; I didn't attend the wedding. It was a point in my life that I thought I was holding two glass balls: work and life. Now looking back, there are more plastic balls than glass balls, and sometimes, you just have to drop them. You need to know what you want. From the place of today, the meeting was a plastic one. What impact did that have on my career? None. Yes, I've learned through that client and the event that I attended, but that one career opportunity did not define the rest.

We all have these moments when we must choose, and it's on us to choose from our future selves what we want now. From the moment I had my children, I have had enough of missing experiences. This became even clearer during the pandemic, when it became easier to see what was really a priority. I want to be there for pickup and drop-off; that is important to me. No, I do not need to be there every day, but I do want to be there regularly. I want to be there for their recitals and for parent interviews. I now put personal activities in my calendar because I respect what I need. Yes, sometimes something comes up that is also important. But I remember that my life is not waiting for me—I only get one. I will decide on being there and present for these great experiences from a place of my future self, not from a place of someone else's expectations of me. The expectations are yours. What do you want?

IN THE HARD

It was so hard
I was in the doing, in the completing
In the accomplishing
Not realizing I was just meant to BE

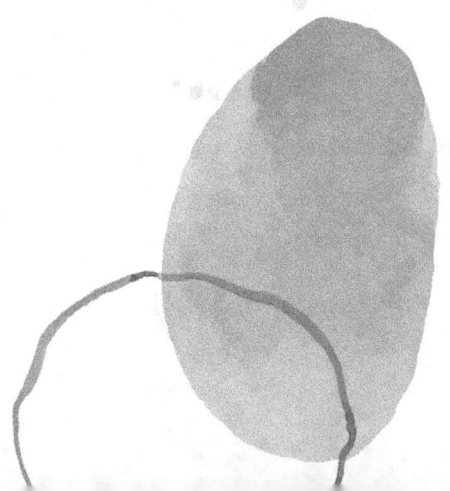

From the time that I started following my intuition, I have truly felt like I do not make bad decisions for myself because in my heart I know the decision for me. I know what I want. What decision needs to be made right when I get the opportunity to decide. The glass balls are never worth dropping. Also, remember that there are a few paths to get to the same destination. Your intuition is presenting the one that is available right now. **When you feel that nudge, I recommend leaning in.** I let intuition make the decision for me. When any experience or opportunity comes about, intuition is choosing the one that's best for me.

I was looking through my journal entries over the years and found one from April 2, 2016. I was at the beginning of my first pregnancy, and I had signed off with: "Note to Self: I'm going to be a powerhouse by thirty-five." It made me smile, this idea of being a powerhouse. I am starting to grow my inner power, and I take the time to respect it. I slow down so that I can hear what that energy has in store for me. **I am not chasing anything because I am already who I need to be. It is in me, and I support the unraveling of this strength.**

What is work and what does it mean to you? That is what I was thinking as I watched this man singing and dancing while putting suitcases on the luggage carousel. He worked at the airport and visibly loved the work he was doing. It was evident to everyone waiting in the security line. I was traveling for a work trip and was surrounded by similarly dressed people, flying for work. People in that room may have been making more than he was, but he was the happiest. This happened many years ago, and I still remember his joy. How we work inspires others. He changed my ideas around work. I didn't understand his feelings at the time, but I do now.

"THE IMPLICATIONS OF A SPIRITUALITY OF WORK ARE CLEAR, IT SEEMS: WORK IS MY GIFT TO THE WORLD. IT IS MY SOCIAL FRUIT-FULNESS. IT TIES ME TO MY NEIGHBOR AND BINDS ME TO THE FUTURE. WORK IS THE WAY I AM SAVED FROM TOTAL SELF-CENTERED-NESS. IT GIVES ME A REASON TO EXIST THAT IS LARGER THAN MYSELF. IT GIVES ME HOPE."

–Joan Chittister, *In the Heart of the Temple*

At dinner, my husband was asked by some friends what his goal was as a teacher. He said: "To be the best teacher in those students' lives."

That statement made me think. What if we all responded that way about our work? What an impact we would all have on one another and future generations. Now that would have a ripple effect.

It doesn't matter if you are the baggage claim worker or the prime minister, we have to take a moment and truly feel grateful for what we get to do. That is the place you work from. Love what you do and where you are. That love is going to influence those around you. It will show you your internal joy.

I don't have to wait until I'm thirty-five to get there, I am already there today. After stopping the chase, I peacefully walk, see nature, and hear the noises of life. It is not perfect every day, but I keep it consistent. When I feel off or not aligned with myself, I know what I need to do to get back to flow with myself. I know the ambience to create a clear headspace. My mat leaves have given me time to discover the next layer of me. Sitting in stillness, in full nothingness, has been a connection to my creative self, my compassionate self, and my loving self. That is the place that I work from. From that place, I can bring clarity to the work I do.

Now, when I live too long in the masculine energy, getting work completed, I feel drained. When I live too long in the feminine energy, of just being, I lose purpose and my energy is low. My body feels content when both are working together. I was in a meeting with a client who had concerns about a project and did not feel heard. I booked a thirty-minute meeting to learn more about their concerns. In that moment, I started the meeting with feminine energy and was an active listener. I took the time to truly hear their needs. I then ended the meeting in masculine energy, where we came up with next steps. They provided a lot of positive feedback after that call. This was the first time I was able to flow between both of my energies.

I gave myself language to describe where I am so I can ask for help when I need it and know when I need to take a break. I have met experts in their field to help me find another piece of the puzzle. That is how I see this journey: box opening and puzzle building—for myself. I am constantly finding out something new about life, about me. I listen to myself and the noises around me. The wind, the birds, the emotions in a room, the emotions in me. That is why journaling is important because you cannot grasp it all until you spill it out on a page. You can then see where your thoughts are headed. You can start piecing it together. Find it for yourself.

MY EULOGY

"Today is the day we say goodbye to Natalia
A mother, loving wife, and inspiring woman.
She saw opportunity and goodness in life's adventures
It was amazing to just stand beside her because she would help you see your own potential
Gave her time and money to various causes to support families, women, her community, and immigrants.
She has been on many stages in her life, but this today will be her last.
I with all the people here impacted by Natalia in her life would like to share my goodbyes.
Her personal legacy and inspiration continue to live in her children and future generations.
Goodbye to a woman who made time to dance and enjoy life
She planted her seeds in the future generations
It is now up to us to water those seeds and keep the garden flourishing for the next generation."

PLANT YOUR SEEDS

1. What is your purpose beyond any role?

_____

_____

_____

_____

_____

_____

2. How can you live tomorrow with more purpose?

_____

_____

_____

_____

_____

3. Keep discovering and rediscovering who you are. Who are you at the core?

_____

_____

_____

_____

_____

4. Describe something you wanted to do as a child but forgot as an adult.

_____

_____

_____

_____

_____

_____

_____

5. At the end of your life, what do you want to hear in your eulogy? Write your own eulogy and live life from that place.

_____

_____

_____

_____

_____

_____

_____

_____

_____

INTUITIVELY YOU

Listen to what is already in your heart
You know your potential
What is out there for you
Waiting for you!
All you have to do is listen
Listen to that voice
You already know everything you need to know
You already have all your tools
Activate it
You have it all
You know what you need to do.

WHAT DOES YOUR VOICE SOUND LIKE?

Intuition is about listening to what's already in your heart. You already know what your potential is, what is out there for you to take or activate. You have to listen to that voice. It's not about learning a new task or doing another program. You already have all the tools you need—you just have to hear it. Stop and be. You have it all, and you know what you need to do. You knew it this whole time. Intuition! That is something I ignored and avoided for many years. Not believing that what is being sent to me has a reason for action. Not realizing that I was supposed to give in and believe it. That is the place from which to make choices, it is not my decision, it already *is*. Explore what intuition looks like for you and feel those daily nudges.

One time during confession, I received authentic advice. I told the priest my sins, and he asked why I did it. I said, "Because of stress that led to a lack of control of my feelings."

Then he asked a good question: "What are you doing to control it?"

He was on to something with that question. *What am I doing?* Now, looking back, I had time to reflect and see that I needed to reach that inner calm, that inner control. For me, I thought it was about searching for more time for silence, when really it was about finding the silence among the everyday, the chaos, the routine.

Another piece, that only came to light recently, was that I now respect myself, so I respect my time. Using the weekends, evenings, and early mornings, not only to do work or cross things off my to-do list, but to spend time in my own silence. Spending time with myself, without being busy. I stopped busying myself. Let the day be filled with peace, quiet, and family time. I made time to spend time with myself because only then do I make time to truly listen to my intuition.

Three moments for Me. When I connect with my intuition, I follow these three steps. I can then hear all the paths in front of me. Intuition leads me with the internal nudges.

1. **Stop.** Take a moment to pause. It quiets down the busy and focuses inward. Feel when you have to stop what you are doing to listen to the message.

2. **Breathe.** With the breath, you go deep down. It shows the here and now. Nothing else matters but the in and out. It allows you to sit in your knowing.

3. **Listen.** The Universe has a message, or it's a moment to ask the Universe for guidance. You will feel the space expand; it connects you to a bigger idea. Yes, you are here and now, and at the same time you are in the future. In the next step. It provides clarity to the action about to be taken.

I started loving myself and what I had to offer. This was not a one-day big eureka moment, but it was a series of small aha moments that left me with an idea of who I truly am. That YOU is right there and within reach. You have to let her out. Move out of the way and away from fear, doubts, and insecurities, and she will emerge. In the everyday joys and experiences, she will smile back at you, and you will be her more and more. Until you have no other options but to commit to her 100 percent. That is when your body and mind are in check. I know the days when I am aligned. My emotions and intuition are clearly connected to my mind and logical thought. You need to let them both be in harmony in order to not get overwhelmed by either one. When you are not aligned, you feel it immediately in the overwhelm.

When I was a child, I stood in front of a large image of Jesus at the front of my church. He winked at me—a spiritual wink. This gave me goosebumps, and I nudged my cousin to ask her if she saw anything. To this day, I still remember the day that Jesus winked at me. It's the same with your intuition; it winks at you every day. From the smallest to the biggest moments, intuition is showing you when to say no, keep going, or wait. Sometimes it is not a time to make a decision; you stop and stay there. There are moments when waiting is the best option.

On Saturday, September 18, 2021, I started asking my intuition questions, through my pendulum. They were specifically yes or no questions. These were questions like:

1. Do I have lettuce in my fridge? *NO (this was my truth testing question that I asked to start. I did not have lettuce in the fridge that day; it was time to go grocery shopping.)*

2. Will I own more companies? *YES*

3. Will my sister and her husband have a baby boy? *YES*

4. Do I drink enough water? *NO (this is true, and my naturopath would agree with me.)*

5. Is my grandmother (Baba) trying to communicate with me? *YES*

6. Does she want to tell me about her life? *NO*

7. Does she want to tell me about her marriage? *NO*

8. Does she want to tell me about her kids? *NO*

9. Does she want to talk about my aunt? *NO*

10. Does she want to talk about my uncle? *NO*

11. Does she want to tell me about my father? *YES*

12. Is he healthy? *YES*

13. Is it about work? *NO*

14. Is it about money? *YES*

15. Does he have enough money? *YES*

16. Is it about his investments? *NO*

At that moment, I took a breath and grounded myself. This was the recommendation I got from my intuitive mentor. Immediately, I knew what it was about. I'd been getting these large visions about what our project would look like, that we were supposed to do this together. I was listening.

17. Are we supposed to work together? *YES*

18. Are we supposed to build what I envisioned? *YES*

Done! I had been trying to have this conversation with my father for weeks. I had been feeling my grandmother for the last week. After my aunt passed away, I immediately said, "My grandmother died around the same age." I don't know where that came from. I went to my dad to ask more about it, and sure enough, they were both sixty-three. Here I was on Saturday night, connecting with my dead grandmother. I was happy to connect with this woman I could not remember because I was so young when she passed away. I felt her presence and her love.

19. After this project is complete will you still be around? *YES*

I felt full! This was the first external technique I used to ask questions, and I was finding it very effective. And still I had no lettuce in the fridge.

20. Should I go grocery shopping tomorrow? YES (our fridge really was quite empty.)

Remember, you do not need a pendulum, you already intuitively know the answer. This is a grounding activity to keep you connected.

* * *

Recently, I heard about Oracle cards. They are spiritual cards used for self-reflection. I went online to search them and find a deck that spoke to me. And I did immediately, one by Tosha Silver. Then I researched her and saw that she's published several books. While researching them, I found my sign. The cover of her book *Outrageous Openness: Letting the Divine Take the Lead* features a winking Goddess statue. I knew I was on the right track. Just like that, I promised my intuition I would not stop listening and that I would have fun with this. The necklace I used for my pendulum, which was my favorite as it was gifted to me by my husband, was going to stay close.

The next day, I decided to choose my weekly fantasy football lineup with the pendulum. I was committed to this new technique. I even benched one of my players, Jonathan Taylor, because my pendulum said so. When my brother-in-law, who manages our league, called me and suggested I play Taylor, I told him: "No, not this week." He was surprised and hesitantly agreed.

I wrote out all the games for Sunday and used my pendulum to decide who was going to win each matchup and sent it to my family as a confirmation. I knew they would keep me honest. Well, my score was not impressive: 5/14. I had to laugh, realizing that maybe this technique should not be used for gambling. I made a mental note for next time.

* * *

Yesterday was my sister's birthday, and she had a group of friends over. I came with my family planning to leave at 6:30 p.m. so that the boys could have a bath and a good night's sleep. We ended up leaving at 9:00 p.m. I was drawn into the potency of intuitive conversations. All night people shared their intuitive nudges and stops. They told me how their decisions were made. During these conversations, I understood I was truly present, then additional puzzle pieces came out of the conversations. People shared their experiences and information with me. This also can impact me. It was the beginning of me becoming an intense conversationalist. I can now speak to a stranger for an hour because they are sharing their deepest feelings. I respect my conversations.

I am feeling my intuition grow stronger by the day. When I go into the fridge, intuition talks to me. On my walks, my intuition tells me which way to turn, when to stop, and when to focus on something else. On Wednesday morning, while getting my boys ready for drop-off, they wanted to wear thinner hats and running shoes. They'd never done that before, but I thought it was supposed to be cold like the rest of the week, so I gave them thicker accessories. It turned out to be a warm day. As I drove to work, I grasped that I didn't listen to *their* intuition: "Universe, noted for next time!"

You are going to be guided with the conversations you participate in. You will know. You are opening up space for yourself. When you come from this place of fullness, you hold space for yourself and your family. Then information and nudges come your way. It is as if you are in a cocoon and it starts to open. I am starting to see more about myself and what I have to offer. The wings are beginning to expand and take up space.

During my first mat leave, I journaled over the first couple of months after my son was born, with messages to my son, myself, or my husband. I needed to get out of my head and release some of the things I was holding onto. I needed to take a break from those thoughts. There were days that were overwhelming. Journaling kept everything in perspective. It helped me feel gratitude. Now, looking at them five years later, I wanted to highlight gratitude.

MY JOURNAL LETTERS

Dear Oldest,
Happy Valentine's Day! My favorite holiday. I love celebrating our love for one another and feeling special. It's a great way to bring together everyone that you love. You don't have to spend a lot of money. Strawberries and raspberries will do. This holiday, I wanted to tell you that I absolutely love you in a way that I haven't loved anyone before you. You are a piece of me. You mean the world to me. When you smiled yesterday and today, I absolutely melted. Every moment with you is special and unique. You change all the time.
Love, Mama

Dear Self,
I will get a job that I enjoy because I now know what I like and dislike. I better understand my strengths and weaknesses. I know what I want to feel. The main concern is leaving the baby, not being there for special moments, not being there to kiss him throughout the day. I keep thinking it is about quality time. Being truly present. When I come home, celebrating his day, listening to any struggles, playing, and bathtime. I still get to be a part of it.
Love, Me

Being a mama, a wife, a daughter, a woman, an employee, an entrepreneur, a community member, a leader, etc., you can forget that the most important being is that person you are within. Make time to find the true you and what you want to bring out into the world. That is going to make all the difference. Do not hide her away—liberate her from the weight on her shoulders. You can be who you want to be every day! Follow the flow and the rhythm of your day. Be one with those feelings. Be the person you truly are. What a gift that would be. It is in those daily small acts that we begin to change and see the beauty that has been there the whole time. It is right inside of you—it is right in front of you!

On Friday, October 1, I went to a bookstore with my sister. Now when I walk in somewhere, I try to be present and see what comes. As I walked in, I noticed Barack Obama's latest book and *The Alchemist*. I thought about my own "personal legend" and began to feel connected to my purpose. While she went to speak with the cashier about a return, I went in search of a notebook but didn't find anything that was meant for me. I then looked at the books near the checkout line and saw a book about a multigenerational farm. I knew I was on the right track. Something caught my eye: *The Happiest Man on Earth* by Eddie Jaku, a Holocaust survivor. I opened the book to Chapter 11 and instantly felt grounded.

"THERE ARE ALWAYS MIRACLES IN THE WORLD, EVEN WHEN ALL SEEMS HOPELESS. AND WHEN THERE ARE NO MIRACLES, YOU CAN MAKE THEM HAPPEN. WITH A SIMPLE ACT OF KIND-NESS, YOU CAN SAVE ANOTHER PERSON FROM DESPAIR, AND THAT MIGHT JUST SAVE THEIR LIFE. AND THIS IS THE GREATEST MIRACLE OF ALL."

—Eddie Jaku

I knew I had to buy the book after that chapter. As I joined the line to pay, I saw my sister was talking to a friend of hers, someone I had never met. She recently had her third child after a long gap between the first two. She said, "I feel like a first-time parent but with the knowledge."

My internal reply was: "I hear you, Universe!" Her message was for me. I'd been thinking about trying for another child, but the timing didn't seem right. Hearing her statement, I knew I had to release the idea that there was an ideal age gap between siblings—and ideal timing. I had to trust that it would happen when it was meant to. I released my internal expectations. I gave in to the flow of life and decided it would happen when it was supposed to. I left the bookstore feeling full and at peace with my ideas. And I had an important new book to read.

A couple of weeks later, I felt another intuitive nudge. I was driving to the bank to sign some papers when I saw a delivery truck driving with its back door all the way up. I could see it was an accident about to happen because the back was full of bread products that he was driving to the next location. I was right behind him; I switched lanes to be safe. Then he changed lanes right in front of me. I honked to get his attention. Nothing. We stopped at a red light, I jumped out of my car, and banged on the side of the truck as I ran to his window. "You're open," I yelled as I pointed to the rear. He thanked me and pulled over to the side of the road to close the door.

At that moment, I thought about my mom and my coach. I remember often telling my mom as a child, "You know you do not have to take action all the time."

And she would reply: "Of course, I had to."

Whether it was a kid getting bullied, someone dropping something on the sidewalk, or someone's car lights not working, she acted with urgency. I then heard my coach's voice in my head telling me: "Make quick decisions."

For most of my life, I did not make decisions quickly or easily. I had to think things through or ask someone for their opinion. Never acting or saying what came to mind even if it needed to be heard. As I was running up to this driver, I knew I had changed. I was now a person who took action. Everyone benefits when you become a quick decision maker with action.

I am now aware of what my parents and grandparents were telling me all this time about feeling a responsibility for their community when they saw something out of place. I now know it is my responsibility to change the outcome. That is my role in the solution. And it's one I gladly accept. *Why not me?* But I first had to find my voice and know how to use it. I upped the volume on my voice.

I took my son to play in the park with his friend. This was a gift to him and quickly it became a gift for myself. I chatted with his friend's mother about the pandemic, being a mama, having boys, and family support. Sitting on this bench chatting about the ease we felt entering motherhood again, unlike the first time. We talked about the fears we felt: someone taking care of your child, being a mama bear, and our constant stress. The more I talk to mothers, the more I see the beauty and challenges it offers. The challenges come from our own expectations of ourselves. I feel that all these mamas support me, too, with their listening and encouraging words. We all need more bench chats at the park, sitting in nature, especially mama bears!

There are moments in this journey when my brain gets excited with more ideas and keeps sending me more—even when my plate is full. I was at my in-laws for Sunday dinner and my father-in-law asked me if I was doing any physical activity that would help with all these ideas. He said I needed to avoid burnout or general health problems and suggested running. My in-laws are very active, so this was not an odd suggestion. Both my husband and brother-in-law are runners, and I agreed with the suggestion. The next morning after dropping my eldest at the bus stop, dropping off my coat at home, and putting on a hat, I was ready for winter running. What a release. *Universe, I needed to run.* Do something for you! Something to release and trust in the process of life, intuition, and self-discovery.

As I was running, I recognized it was hard to think about anything other than running. I ran less than two kilometers and eventually stopped thinking where I wanted to get to and instead created check-points in my head. I picked a location, then when I got there, I'd pick the next spot. At that moment, I had another breakthrough: we need to break down the big dreams and goals in this way. **It can be stressful thinking about the destination. You just need to think about the incremental gains you'll make on your way there—that is how you will get there.**

I was listening to a podcast about female sexuality. They stated that the most spiritual experience was the process of being pregnant. Something that was never there before, now is, and it takes form, becomes a human. Did my womb wake me up to the world? Did it make me see the energy around me? Did my womb activate something in me other than having the baby?

Here I am! I have met my deepest and most intuitive self. The one who can unlock the unseen. That can only be seen with my soul. It has been here the whole time. I now see the skills I can use. My husband and I have started connecting differently because we are grounded in ourselves. The pandemic has brought us back to ourselves. To that being who is grounded, who knows what is most important—you.

Let me go back to the beginning of the year. I was having a lot of women ask me about my intuitive mastermind, which I had just launched. Prior to that I offered a free intuitive workshop to see the level of interest for this program. In November, I launched my "Mama Mastermind." Here I was at the beginning of November, intuitively knowing that I would be launching this program for mamas. Mamas looking to explore their abilities, which were waiting to come out.

In mid-November, I shared the first mastermind. I already saw it in my mind as being successful. I believed I could do it because I saw it. No one was formally registering, but the DMs kept filling up with people's positive commentary. Their experiences as a mother with their child, their changing body, partnership, self, and more. It was coming in, and I was being seen as the person to go to discuss these topics. I felt it. I felt what the Universe wanted me to feel! That it was me who was supposed to do this. I was on the right path. A path of abundance. I was being led from the heart and speaking from that same place.

Leading up to the day, more and more people kept contacting me. But no one registered, not even one. I kept smiling because I knew it was irrelevant if someone did because the learning was for me. For me to understand my role and abilities.

The Universe was leading me all year. I knew it would show me a compelling message. On December 6, the program launched a feeling inside of me like I was on cloud nine, even though no one was in the program. A lot of people came to me with positive feedback: "I love your content, but I'm not a mom." They felt they could only join the program if they were moms. I knew I needed to open it up to others.

Then my social media team suggested that I offer something free at the end of the month. I knew exactly what was needed for it to be an intuitive workshop. My intuitive coach kept telling me not to put an attendance limit on the program because a lot of women were interested. They were coming. I told her that I was finally ready to label my offerings as intuitive. I felt like that intuitive being with gifts was me, not just someone in a book. She added: "Natalia, you hold space for these conversations."

Yes, I was seeing it in my DMs. I thought I knew what she meant, but that was only skimming the surface.

The end of December rolled around, and I launched the program. The first day was incredibly powerful. From the very first fifteen minutes, women were sharing from an authentic place. A place of vulnerability, from their raw self. The women did not know one another, but they knew that they needed to be in the room. I knew I needed to be seeing this because most of the women who registered were not mamas. They were women who were ready to crack themselves open to who they truly were. I rebranded my website on day two for all women, not just mothers. I understood what intuition wanted me to do. I created the right space for all women. Then I launched the "Intuitively You" mastermind.

A friend has shared that when she joined the group, she didn't know what she wanted. From that workshop moving forward, she started exploring her purpose and creativity. In the group setting, seeds got planted.

I couldn't wait to see where this took me. As I was editing my website, I kept seeing the mastermind when I looked at it. I was starting to feel this group of women entering my life. This was for them as much as it was for me. That was the gift. We all have intuitive gifts to share with one another. That is where the magic exists. We all benefit when we activate these intuitive gifts.

PLANT YOUR SEEDS

1. What does your inner voice sound like? What does it tell you?

_____

_____

_____

_____

_____

2. How do you release yourself to the process and trust that it will take you where you need to go?

_____

_____

_____

_____

_____

3. What does intuition feel like for you, in your body, mind, and spirit?

_____

_____

_____

_____

_____

4. Describe an intuitive experience you've had. That only makes sense to you.

_____

_____

_____

_____

_____

_____

_____

_____

5. Connect with the Universe and be grateful for the moments to learn and hear something new. You are being exposed to more than meets the eye. What are you grateful for feeling before it even takes form in your life?

_____

_____

_____

_____

_____

_____

_____

_____

_____

_____

SECTION 2

A LIFE OF CREATION

A life of creation is filled with time to create and discover. When you are playful and making space for creativity, big ideas flow your way. It can be as simple as taking a relaxing bath, listening to your favorite song, visualizing, painting, journaling, playing an instrument, walking, or biking.

Many people claim that waking up early is a great idea. During different parts of my life, I tried. I really tried. Somehow, I was always tired and foggy. A big part of that was because I was unfocused. I did not know what future goals I was working toward. I didn't have a clear purpose for myself, for me to want to wake up early. Now, with my morning routine, I know why I am waking up early before my family. I make time for some form of joyful movement, meditation, music, or I appreciate the silence. No matter what my mood was before this moment, I end up with a smile and excitement toward my day.

Ask yourself why you are waking up. What do you want to see and experience in the morning? You will see that in all of this you are making space for those big ideas. You will get more comfortable with the silence. In that silence, there are ideas, messages, and colors. Messages come to us every day—are you listening? Are you seeing? Are you feeling? Your morning routine will become a moment for realization and discovery.

After I wrote this section on routine, there were a few changes that happened one morning to mine. I woke up later than usual, was running late preparing breakfast for the family, and didn't end up meditating. My son came down for breakfast and said, "Mama, there is no music!"

I forgot to put on the breakfast instrumental music that had become our norm. Even my young son knew when we were filling the space with all our goodness.

I had made applesauce the night before, and as I was heating it up to go on our oatmeal, the handle broke off the pot. The sticky sauce spilled on the floor and splattered on the cabinets. As I was cleaning it up, I went through my daily gratitude and smiled. I was thankful my husband had vacuumed the night before, so our floors were clean enough that I could save some of the sauce. Then I laughed to myself, thinking that changes to my usual routine will happen, and I love that my days are filled with beauty and abundance. I am forever grateful for what I get to see and experience in this lovely kitchen.

Life is not about tomorrow or next year. It is about today, in the everyday experiences that you will make space to create and plant the seeds of opportunity. Be creative, be imaginative, be excited, be here in the boldness. Welcome to the club. You join simply because you *are*—and the membership is free. I cannot wait to see what you create!

THANK YOU!

Thank you for the moments when I am present, the small every-day ones

Cuddling with my husband on a Wednesday

Watching the basketball draft and seeing their home celebrations as they embrace their family during these proud accomplishments.

The money that flows into my bank account, as well as sending funds to someone else's

Dreams and getting lost in the daydreaming

The clean sink at night with all dishes waiting in the drying rack

The full sink in the morning because it means we had food to eat off the plates

The laundry that gets folded

The laundry that is washed downstairs in the laundry bin

The potty-training successes even on the day filled with accidents

The before-bed dance parties

Naps that give you alone time

Saturday Disney movie days

Saturdays when plants get watered

The fresh basil on the balcony

The kids getting excited about new shoes and accessories

The days you drink water straight from the tap

Going out of the house by yourself

Going for a bike ride with the whole family

Golf lessons with your partner

The advice you give that brings a smile to someone's face

The moment you hear something from a different lens

The review you sent because someone did something that left a smile on your face

The right people you meet along your path

Being happy and grateful now that the small wins are appreciated!

YOUR CREATIVITY

One warm spring day, I finished work and was looking around the house. The main space was not celebrating or supporting the needs we had every day. I started reorganizing. By the time my husband came home, the space had a distinct before and after. The main floor reflected our kids' needs now. It was made for them to play and enjoy. At the same time, it gave all of us space to have our own little corner. It wasn't out of a design magazine, but it had a level of practicality that was reflective of our needs. I am grateful that we live in a home where I can accommodate us now and as our children get older.

Over the last two years, I changed how I do things at home. I used to do things unhappily, quickly, and with stress or anger. With all this new labeling and releasing, I even wash dishes in the morning with more presence and positivity. I feel gratitude in my laundry every time I start a load; I am grateful for all the hours I get back in my day because of my washing machine.

I spoke to a mom friend; we agreed growth in perspective started by accepting the things you cannot control. You accept the chaos from a place of gratitude. Like in the summer, when the schedule for kids changes and you start going with the flow. Bedtime changes, more laundry accumulates, and meals are inconsistent as you spend more time outside of the home.

I am grateful for the opportunity to feel and see more every day.

The previous Christmas season, as a family, we drove around looking at Christmas lights in our neighborhood, something we started doing when the kids were little. We all piled into the car after dinner and experienced all that was offered to us. The ability to disconnect from routine and responsibilities; to be in the enjoyment and be inspired. I absolutely loved driving around and appreciating it together. We now have our list of favorite homes to visit and shared which ones brought us joy.

Again, there's an opportunity to feel more and see more every day. You will begin to appreciate the inspiration that comes your way.

GODDESS

I am my own person
I do things my way
I dance to the beat of my own drum
I know what I want to do
I am rooted in myself, my beliefs, my offerings.
I define my own femininity, the one on the inside which reflects on the outside
I do not get pulled into different directions, I stay true to my motivations
I know who I am and I love myself.
These roots hold me, keep me here
I am the Mother of the Universe
I am a protector of me and those around me
Here is my loving embrace.
It is not filled with shoulds or musts
It is filled with my own version, my own truth
I appear as myself as my truest self
I see something bigger in me and those around me
I know my purpose.
This is how I am in my family, my community, the world
I am starting to feel like the mother of the community
This is the energy I have in my home
You may not get what you want, but you will get what you need.
I'm starting to see this in me!

I make time for visualization, writing, journaling, coaching my clients, and working with coaches myself. That does not mean I make time for everything every day, but every day I do make time for something for myself, from five minutes to an hour. I can find something to fill my cup. It doesn't matter what version I create; there is joy in the smallest and biggest version of something. They both have much to offer to me. My morning practice begins with preparing breakfast for my family and putting the clean dishes away. There is meditative or chanting music in the background while I light some candles and calmly complete the tasks. I feel full and abundant by 7 a.m. I now appreciate the significance of a morning routine. I found a version that works for me. That gets me excited for my day and my goals.

I know I am doing my 1 percent each day to build toward those goals through this routine, so by the time December 31 rolls around, I have created something. It doesn't have to be big to mean something. Something bigger than me and my every day. I do not wait for things to happen; they come to me when I am ready. There are things I said no to in order to make space for this: no news and no social media first thing in the morning. Eliminate the distractions; it is just noise that is distracting you from your inner reason by removing precious time.

I became a writer during my morning routine. I did not label myself this way prior to this year. I aspired to write but didn't see it in my near future. I loved journaling and writing poetry as a child and teen. I thought it was a retirement project, something I would start up when I had time and fewer distractions. One day I was on a video call with my coach. As I entered a breakout room, someone asked if I was a children's writer. My husband is an elementary school teacher, and we had set up the basement with a book wall for his online teaching and for our boys during the lockdowns. As she said this, I thought to myself: "Universe, I hear you."

In the debrief that day, I said the impact her words had on me, and I saw myself writing again. Then another participant sent me my current publisher's information, encouraging me to book a discovery call. Something that I thought was only a wish set itself up for me. All I had to do was say YES. So, I did. I now put writer in my personal introductions. I accept that. This is no longer a wish. I became a writer with a constant morning routine and that is how I came to write this book, as well as plan for future pieces.

My art journey has been interesting. I have been drawn to music and art my entire life, but I never saw myself as the creator of this work. I always saw someone else doing it and me appreciating the offering. I never saw this as my talent. Yet, here I am. Taping my work to the wall and putting together a creative desk in my bedroom where I take the time to connect within and produce something bigger than me every day.

I still remember playing the trumpet in grade nine music class. I was by far the worst in the class; I am not exaggerating. I knew all the notes, but I could not hit any of them. I also didn't practice playing the instrument. I didn't get to the point of making it a habit, making it my norm. In that class, I worked on a project about Billie Holiday, and I fell in love with jazz. I cannot forget her voice, the heaviness of her songs. That course changed my thinking about music, the depth of music, and how it can get into your soul. It was a great opportunity to enjoy something and at the same time not be able to do it well. It was a humbling experience.

A creative output is a dynamic way to communicate our needs, our wants, and our potential. How can we help this important part of our imagination flourish, regardless of resources? How do we let it represent our ever-changing selves?

We often criticize social media for the addiction it has become in all our lives, but I recently learned of its beauty. I launched my Mama Mastermind for the first time. Here I thought that the gift was sharing this community with other mothers. Instead, mamas contacted me and shared their stories about their spouse, body, baby, emotions, perseverance, culture, etc. Here I was feeling the true gift of launching was for me to create the space for these one-on-one conversations. Mamas being able to message me about their reality. I felt the gift of social media and having a creative outlet. I shared my story to then be given the opportunity to listen to others.

As the month went on, I decided I was ready for a giveaway. I spoke with a local beauty product company, created by a group of women, and they were interested in working together. I launched this giveaway, with the support of my social media team and paid for an additional boost so it could reach a wider audience. The love and support kept coming with a constant flow of positive energy. Then I hopped onto Instagram to respond to a few messages and saw that a woman from California shared my latest blog. A poem about motherhood. My name was on the post and there were all my words. This was a poem I wrote for myself and it resonated. It brought tears to my eyes seeing the significance of personal creativity. Creativity is an outlet for ourselves, but we all benefit.

AND . . .

Motherhood shows you the ANDs of life:
You understand that life can be challenging and lead to growth
It is draining and inspiring
A day can be loud and peaceful
A week can be long and short
You can be sad and feel joy
You can feel accomplished and still search for your place in the world
You can be having a pleasant family moment and have meltdowns from the kids
You are patient and have too much
You can be at peace and have crazy all around you
You can make food and not cook today
You can be a leader and not know your path
You can be receiving and not want to give right now
You can be giving and not want to receive
The days that feel perfectly aligned and were not perfect
You are tired and you wake up
Your life can be messy and organized
Sometimes your house is messy and messier
Overall, you love and more love happens
You are a mother and an individual
You can give to yourself and your children.
The AND of life is what I've been observing
I can be creative and structured
I am empowered and exhausted
I can be level-headed and emotional
I am all of this and more
Thank you, Universe, for showing me the beauty of life and the everyday!

In one of my hypnotherapy sessions, the practitioner said: "Keep writing your poetry." This was not something she knew about me; it was something she felt. I knew what she meant as I was also feeling the need to ramp up my poetry. After her intuitive message, I knew that poetry would be in this book and would show up on my blog more often. What is a creative outlet that draws you in? Make time to work on it every day. We will all benefit from your creative work.

When you heal and take the time to forgive yourself, your past will transform. You will be curious about today, about the present. Your interactions with your partner, your kids, your family, and even complete strangers will change. You are holding space for a different energy, for a different environment. You unlock your abilities, your power, and your flow. The word "bold" is exactly the word to summarize what unleashed creativity does to all this internal knowing. When I opened myself to thoughts and ideas, as well as sat in my silence, I met the bigger, fuller, and louder me. I found groups of women who were exploring their own boldness. Groups where we could share this and be supported. Bold has become my favorite word. Whenever I lose sight of myself and my abilities, I repeat the word to myself. I feel it in the conversations I join, the control I have over my inner energy. I am no longer waiting on the sidelines of my life. I am in it! I now celebrate the little moments and the big achievements. They are all worth noticing. I am doing it for me from this place of gratitude. Others benefit when my own cup is overflowing, I share the excess that I create. All I truly seek is to be guided to the fullest and truest me! I keep getting closer by leaning into this bold me.

I initially began writing this book to coincide with my intuitive coaching business. Along the way, it became a thank-you letter to motherhood, to womanhood, to my kids, and to myself. I love who I have become through my new experiences. My oldest and I watercolor together, learn the piano together. There is a lot of discovery for both of our creative selves. When you keep having these ideas and thoughts, you will accept the form it will take. Keep being curious.

I started a watercolor painting course that shares the importance of creating a "sacred space" for our art, our creation. One Thursday evening, that is exactly what I did. I ordered my white desk with metallic gold legs and piled up some notebooks, books, plants, and candles. I created a special space for myself. A place that inspires, calms, and excites me. My oldest woke up in the morning, looked, and asked when he was getting his own desk. He is watching and mimicking my every move. By understanding my true personal purpose, I demonstrate that to him. I need to know why I am doing what I am doing so that when he asks, I have a reason. An explanation. The next day, I prepared his creative desk.

PLANT YOUR SEEDS

1. How can you stay in the being a little longer?

   _____

   _____

   _____

   _____

   _____

2. Explore your boldness. What is coming out for you after reading this chapter? Doodle it, draw it, write it, explore it!

   _____

   _____

   _____

   _____

   _____

3. Describe something that awakens your five senses and makes your soul smile.

   _____

   _____

   _____

   _____

   _____

4. When do you feel the most creative?

_____

_____

_____

_____

_____

_____

_____

_____

5. What is a creative piece you can unleash in yourself every day?

_____

_____

_____

_____

_____

_____

_____

_____

_____

_____

_____

GAINING A NEW PERSPECTIVE

"TO LIVE IS THE RAREST THING IN THE WORLD. MOST PEOPLE EXIST, THAT IS ALL."
—Oscar Wilde

A big part of my early adulthood life was running away from these feelings and emotions. Not realizing that what I was running away from was a part of me. I saw this in my unhealthy relationship with alcohol. It was really exposed to me during my first pregnancy when I comprehended how much I craved a glass of wine at the end of the day. I craved it for the ability it had to make me run from what was in my head. While I was pregnant with my first, I promised myself to enjoy a drink from a different place after I had the baby. I no longer wanted to drink to drain or remove but to enjoy and to celebrate.

When I started working with my intuition after my second pregnancy, I again struggled with drinking but from a different lens. Even one drink fogged my brain so my intuition did not nudge in the same way the next day. There is a level of clarity in my body that I seek now. Patterns and rhythms that are a part of me. I have taken responsibility for my drinking, and it has freed me. Freed me to choose from a place of fullness, gratitude, and celebration. As with every learning, I am humbled to experience growth and to be able to notice the difference in me. Here I stand with the utmost gratitude.

This year, I have been in search of self-love and internal peace. I have been reading books, visualizing, doing yoga, biking, praying, reflecting, journaling, listening to music, dancing, and painting. When I started to see it in myself then I started seeing it in others. My husband's name means "love and peace." Only this year did I see I had it here in our house and our hearts, this whole time. I was missing it! It is when I started noticing my husband as a calm, peaceful, and loving being that I began to truly see and feel it all around. Not just for myself and my boys but for my husband and our community. We have started sharing our spiritual, parenting, and couple journey with each other from this angle of peace and love. When the world slowed down during the pandemic, we gave ourselves grace to slow down with it and notice the little things. When that happened, there was a readiness to explore the bigger things in life.

My hardest obstacle to get over was asking for and receiving support. It was hard for me to get out of my own head—and people want to help, even strangers. They truly, from the bottom of their heart, want to improve your life, your day, your hour. My in-laws offered help with gardening, cleaning, caregiving, and cooking. For instance, when we drive over to their home, they will come outside and offer to take our boys. I was used to doing everything myself and held onto the idea that I could do everything, that I couldn't even receive their support. It was free and available, and I still could not say yes. I would say no and carry everything. Over time, I appreciated that even though I could carry everything, I didn't need to—I can receive the support others want to give me.

At the airport, while traveling with my sister and our three boys, a stranger came up to us to ask if we needed help. After doing this self-work, I've noticed help comes and you have to lean in. I asked if he could take the stroller to the airplane. We were still sweating getting onto the airplane, but we had one less thing to drag along with us. After we landed, he got off the plane, grabbed the bag and carried it into the airport for us. Another woman, who was traveling with her husband and child, helped pull my carry-on to the sitting area. I was being kinder to myself by receiving. It did not cost anything; I had to say yes. Now, when someone messages me about an opportunity to grow myself, my business, my ideas, I stop and listen to the offering. It's the Universe leaving me a message. It might not always look the way that I thought it would, but it would be available if I was ready to receive it. We are so used to saying no or not yet because we imagine it differently. And fear gets in the way of activating these exciting projects that sometimes fall into our lap. Say yes if that pull or that nudge is there. It is there for you to embrace and take on.

I was at the mechanic thinking back to all the times I was open to receiving from my family, friends, strangers, and the Universe and feeling quite proud. Then as I was driving home, I stopped to get a couple iced coffees, one for me and one for my husband, who was working from home. I also added a bagel. The wonderful server offered a tray, and I automatically said no. I thought it was better for the environment. As I was walking to the car, I started thinking that I did not want to spill them. I made it into the car without a problem, but once I was home and walking up to the door, I dropped them and spilled the sticky drinks all over the front door. I laughed as my husband opened the door to all of this. I forgot to receive; all I could think was: "Universe, I'm sorry I didn't listen." From that point forward, I vowed to receive from everyone. Remember, when someone is offering to help, say yes and don't fight it.

My friend wanted to organize my branding photoshoot, but I already had this fancy one planned in my head. She said, "I understand what you want and would be happy to do this for you."

I went with her idea, and it was wonderful. She gave me a person-alized photoshoot with stand-in models and a vision for my social media. My brand ideas expanded that day with all of this positive energy. She understood my brand and how I was looking to grow. It was the best investment because she customized everything to me. She cared and that reflected in every aspect of the day. We then had brunch to celebrate and plan the social media strategy. It was amazing, and I felt grateful.

The following week, as we were driving from our in-laws, my oldest said, "Mama, my bucket is full!"

I knew exactly what he meant. My heart swells with gratitude, peace, and trust. I wrote out my daily gratitude list and signed off: *I could keep going . . . only gratitude. Thank you, Universe, God, Spirit, Goddesses, Ancestors, Archangels for the love. For liberating me and showing me that what I thought was my path was only the stepping stones to something greater and bigger, the fullest me.*

As I joined the workforce after finishing at university, I was ready to climb the corporate ladder and join the vertical climb of society. But what's better than all of this? I am now on a horizontal development path, where I deepen my roots and learn more based on where I am. I am exactly where I am supposed to be. It is my time to activate and liberate all my talents through conversations, exploration, and being.

I hold the key, and I unlock my own doors. I have taken responsibility for my past, present, and future. I accept that only I control the outcome. The world is an ever-changing place, but I am my own constant, from the way that I wake up, to the conversations I participate in, to the way I energetically walk into a room; from the way I speak with my family, to how I go to bed with gratitude and peace in my heart.

This was not always the case. I used to live in the hard: I dreaded Mondays, didn't feel like I made enough money, wasn't fully passionate about what I was doing, then I drank too much on the weekend to wash away the week. I let myself be the supporting actress in my own life movie. I did not act like the lead. I let people make decisions and take actions for me. I am no longer available for that. What changed? Many tiny things that made the impact from early morning practice, living from gratitude, visualization, centering prayer, intentional conversations, and motherhood.

What does this perfect day in my one wild and precious life look like? I now wake up with gratitude to have one more day to see and experience. I make time to wake up slowly but deliberately. I shower and smell the scents of the soap and the creams. I put on my robe, get dressed, and go downstairs to do movement, to get my body prepared for the day. Afterward, I make time to write, ponder, and explore topics that come to me. Then I prepare breakfast and lunches for the family, again, from a place of gratitude and fullness because I have food to give them. I am grateful to have dishes to wash and to have a roof over my head. I am grateful to be surrounded by purposeful energy and people.

Not everyone loves routine. During my first mat leave, I found my days incredibly repetitive and predictable. I felt like too many of them were exactly the same. They all blended into one. Now, I embrace this routine; it brings me such joy. I wake up, have time for me and my ideas, time to write and move my body. Then as the boys wake up, I prepare breakfast and tea. We leave room for the unpredictable, but so much joy is in the regular everyday moments. There is the predictability of daycare and bus drop-off. I work with joy and precision while being in my quiet home. Then I prepare soup and dinner. I enjoy getting food ready for the family, so we can have a meal together. I spend time with my eldest while we wait for the other two. We practice piano, letters, or numbers. We end our day with dessert, a dance party, bathtime, then reading before bed. We then sleep and move into the next day. I love my days and the gifts they bring along.

The rest of my day ebbs and flows. I allow for flexibility; I am not only controlled by timelines and completion dates. I am moved by excitement, opportunity, and the unknown. I do not say yes because I must but instead because I want to. The people who I meet are sending me intuitive nudges or new messages. As I like to say, they are giving me my next box. Be playful to those unknowns, and do not be dragged down by these undiscovered elements. This is not how I used to see myself, but I like this version of me.

DAILY PRACTICE

Be BOLD
Be Me
Just BE
Do more of that
The feel goods, the do goods, radiate good.
Stay connected to you
TRUST
RELEASE
LET GO.
Move through the journey
In FLOW
In YOU
In the ENERGY.
Be Present
Enjoy the journey
It only happens once!

I was waking up my oldest early one morning to get him ready for Baba and Dido's (Grandma and Grandpa in Ukrainian). He was excited to spend Sunday morning with them in their alluring yard, go on a picnic, and see their new kittens. I was giving him an apple to eat before getting to Baba's. As I was passing the apple to him, he immediately looked at me and asked if I could cut it into slices. It was immediate. At that moment, I was mesmerized by the immediacy. As adults, we lose that. I know I did. Knowing exactly what I want while I am in the moment. To be able to give it words and an explanation right then. Not when I walk away from the situation.

The whole day, I thought about this experience. When do we lose that confidence in ourselves? Why do we forget to put our needs first as moms, as women? Like on the airplane, why are we not putting the metaphoric air mask on ourselves first before we help others? It's my kids who are showing and teaching me. I need to pause long enough to see it and appreciate it. See what has been in front of me this whole time.

I used to come from a place where things had to be challenging. Now, the more I lean into gratitude, the more enjoyable life has become. When something is being completed, I enjoy the journey and the emotions and actions come with ease. I noticed a big difference when I was potty training my youngest. The difference between the first time and the second time around is that I used to live in a place with hard rules. With my second, I still leaned on similar ideas and concepts that I read about the first time, but I wove them in with my intuition.

I read my younger son's signs to see what he needed and when he was ready. In the end, I spent more time seeing his growth and enjoying the journey of potty training. His incremental wins made me smile. I'd go to bed grateful for his potty-training accomplishments, and it was a lovely family experience.

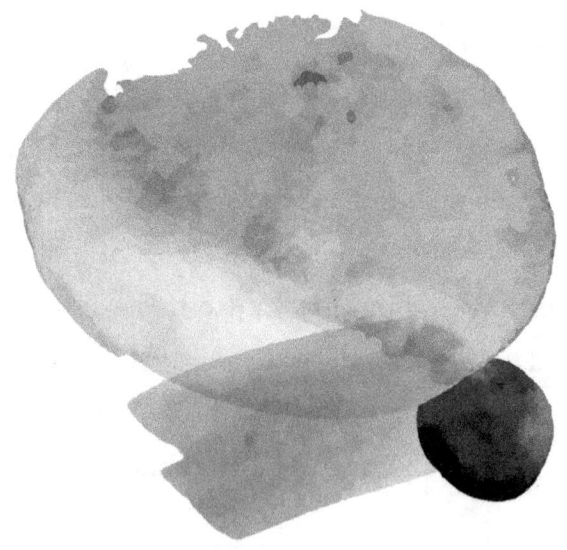

FORGIVENESS

I forgive myself
For all those moments I held onto for days, weeks, or even years.
I forgive myself
I love myself
For those moments, I walked away with that feeling.
I forgive myself
Those moments do not define me
I do not need to be perfect to move forward.
I need to forgive
I remove that cloud hanging over my head, and I release that hold on my body, mind, and heart.
I am a woman who lives each day with purpose
Even when the day is less than perfect
I offer my love and gratitude.
I walk away from my fears
They do not define me.
The more love I give myself
The more people around me feel my never-ending energy
My abundance fills me first, then those around me.
I offer this to myself from this day forward
I feel life, source, Universe, Spirit, God pulling me forward.
I know when to lead and when to follow
I know that with this intuitive guidance the world will gift me with full days from my full heart.
Universe, oh how I love you!

Today, I had a great conversation with my sister and dad in his kitchen about forgiveness. We've realized that people who need your attention will show it to you in some way. It is all tied back to the depth of being a community member. At the core of it is the importance of taking care of yourself first. That's step one of being a community member. Step two is you go a bit bigger and you support your immediate family, the people in your actual home. Once you've taken care of yourself and you've really filled your own cup, then you can go to the next layer, and the layer after that is your family outside of your home. Once you've got that, it's your friends, then it's your community members, and it gradually expands.

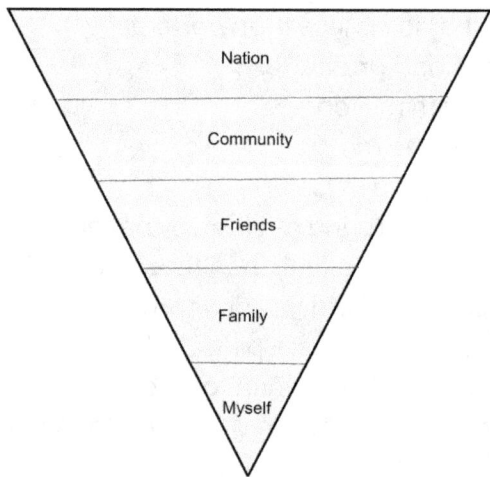

I shared with them my emotional cup that I imagine as a blue teacup with an embroidery pattern that I have in my home. Once my teacup is overflowing, I am then ready to go to the next level of care, kindness, love, and compassion. Only then do I have something to give. It's not about going to that person and giving them something, it is about you being grounded and rooted in who you are. You can then give from that place. Someone else comes with their teacup and they skim it along your overflowing cup. I got home and imagined a pyramid of sparkling champagne glasses, the ones that are piled up on top of one another, like I've seen in movies. That's what it is like, when you pour that champagne to the first top glass, and it flows down into the others.

You keep doing your self-work and ground yourself in your values. The people that see your work are going to come in and want to be part of your champagne pyramid. You will inspire from this place. You will inspire your partner/spouse and your kids. You don't have to go and tip it into their mug. They'll know when they want in. That's the place to give from. Where you don't even have to go outside of yourself to give it. You just need to be who you truly are, at your best loving, kind, and compassionate self. You become love in its truest purest sense.

There was so much I didn't know about my maternity leave the first time around. I didn't know about the level of exhaustion, the recovery time for myself, the breastfeeding pain, the change in my relationship with my husband, and the need for support. We need space to learn, to uncover, to be. With the second maternity leave, I left space for myself. And I was able to learn who I am and who I want to be. I created time for myself.

It was a major change when my youngest started daycare, especially after being at home during lockdowns with both my husband and me working from home. All month, he cried. It had been the four of us for such a long time in his life. He comes home with big hugs for us every evening. His love language is physical touch, which is very evident when he is upset or having a difficult time. That's when he needs extra hugs and kisses. In his experience, I reminded myself that we all need time to cope with change. **The more you do the work, the less time you will need, but you still need time. Be kind to yourself.**

I'm realizing the more my son looks at my actions and asks me the big questions of life, the more important it is that I'm authentic. I give him the gift of authenticity. I live my own authentic life, where I get to ask the big questions of life's meaning. It's what I choose to do in my morning routine, the conversations I participate in, the activities I do, and the love that I give to myself and others. Discover this for yourself.

He is regularly telling me the projects we will do together. He knows we can do it all, just not everything today or this year. I finally started believing that and seeing it for myself. He now sees it for the both of us. I radiate goodness from this place. I enter a room differently, and he sees that even when I think he is not looking. He sees me making time for my passions. He now also wants to paint and to write. On my path of self-discovery, he is walking alongside me and discovering for himself.

* * *

In the fall, I was hopping onto a Zoom call with one of my friends to discuss some of the projects we were working on and looking to organize a project together. We started chitchatting when suddenly my left hand and left side of my face started tingling and I didn't have exact control of my movement. I wanted it to go left, and it didn't quite listen. I told her I was not feeling well and having these odd symptoms. Then, my tongue started feeling odd and I could not control where I placed it as I continued to talk with her. Then my vision started tunneling and the right side of my head started pounding and the headache began. Let me tell you, this was a scary moment. Before this moment, I considered myself a healthy person. In an instant, that can change. I knew why I needed all this self-work to get through this moment.

I was home alone with my son, who had recently come home from school. At that moment, I knew my friend was the only person that could help me in case I needed it. I stayed on the call for an hour and grabbed a glass of water to calm my nerves. I could feel the panic in my body. After thirty minutes, all that was left of my symptoms was a headache on the right side. None of this was normal for me.

My husband came home with our youngest, and I went to the hospital. There was a level of urgency to my stay in emergency. I was well taken care of and supported. They ran tests and kept me overnight. As I was sitting there in the quiet room, I felt gratitude. An unbelievable amount of gratitude. I don't get to choose the end date of my life, but I do, however, get to choose how I live every day until then. I will value future opportunities.

It ended up being migraine auras, which unfortunately have symptoms very similar to a stroke. I had twenty-four hours in a hospital to really think about what I love about life. I had to get out of my everyday life and see the meaning of it all. That the world is my oyster and I get to choose what I do with it. I walked out the next day with a smile on my face and went home to a dinner prepared by our favorite local restaurant and to my kids excited to have a dance party. As always, Life, thank you for one more day.

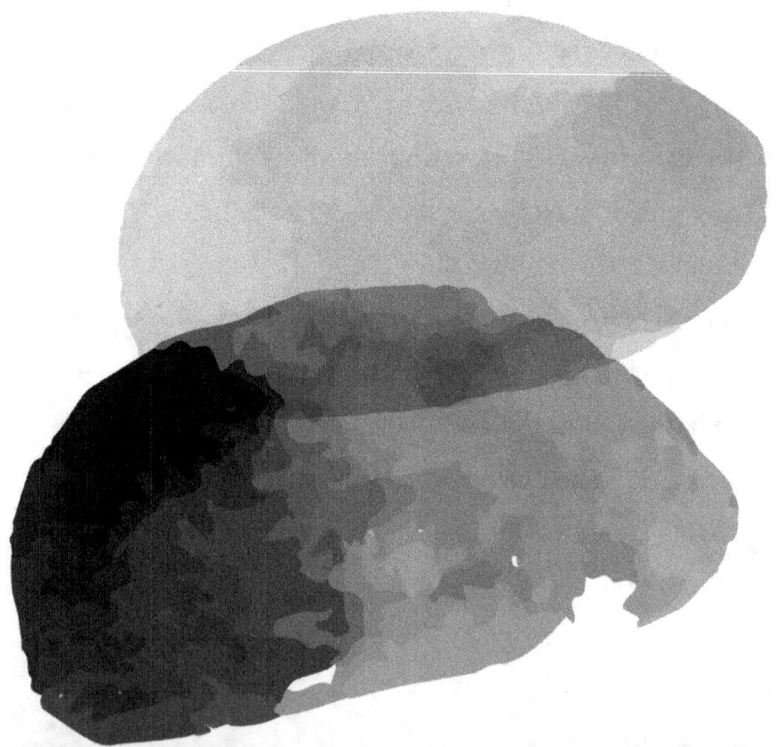

LOVE

Open your heart space and show what you have to offer
We all benefit when you show love
Love for life, for each other.
Be the hands, the love that others need to see
Because you've offered love and gratitude to yourself first
Expand it! There is more, we all have so much to offer
You will draw people in through your heart
Your nonjudgment, your kindness.
It comes full circle, that space you hold, only you can create
We are all blessed by your love
The best version of you embodies love
Show up from the place of love
You are a beacon of love
It buzzes all around you
The Mother Teresa in all of us is waiting to shine.

Now, as a wind down for the day, I celebrate. I celebrate the lovely offerings that came to me. Things I would have missed in the past. For instance, I started seeing:

- Stunning patterns on clothing that make me pause and smile.
- My boys' growth and discovery; they are constantly uncovering something new.
- My husband's ability to look within, to really see the situation for what it is and not falsify his reality.
- For the morning quiet that is there for me to enjoy and sit in. In contemplation, questions, feelings, and so much more. In the morning, I feel I am exactly where I am supposed to be.
- For life's big questions that come out of my son and his imagination. He makes me look inside of myself.

"LIFE PRESENTS YOU WITH LEARNING ONLY WHEN YOU ARE READY TO EXPERIENCE IT."
—Natalia Harhaj

My colleague at work was saying that his kids were excited for their trip and that they could not wait. He was telling them to enjoy the beauty of the days leading to the vacation. I celebrate because I understand today is the only one you have guaranteed. You can only enjoy today.

Motherhood is humbling. That is what I keep saying in conversations with friends and colleagues. It is not about being perfect. If it was, we would never get there. It is about seeing yourself through the eyes of your child. They keep holding the mirror and the question that came up for me was: Is this how I want to be seen? In the beginning, you think you are the parent so you must be the teacher. I am the teacher, the student, and the equal to my 5-year-old. I didn't know that in the process of motherhood, I would be humbly taught, slowed down, and shown that this moment only exists once.

I completed my best running day today. I started running at the end of the year last year. I had no idea that I needed this activity. I needed the release. I needed the feeling that I could do it, during any season. Seeing that I can do whatever I set my mind to because I see the goal at the end of the tunnel. Today I ran four kilometers, and it could have been more. It felt like such a monumental achievement. I ran into the house, and I felt full. It was exactly what I needed. Then I took a bath, a day bath, as my youngest took a nap. I set up my candles, added Epsom salts and some bubbles to the water, and put on some meditative music. Relaxing, it came to me that I had all of these abilities for a reason. When people needed my support, they would find me. I was starting to see a lot of things for other people.

I had a conversation with my husband a couple of years ago about wanting to give our son the tools for support so when he feels like he's lacking something, he knows what he can do for himself. Over the last two weeks, I started running with him. In this process, I needed to run with him to show him what tools I was using. When he started running with us, he would go for one and a half kilometers. We'd drop him back home and continue even further. We were building up the tools that we can share generation to generation.

Every weekend or as he is falling asleep he asks if we are going to run the next day. I wasn't planning on running this often, but here I was going down the path. I now have a junior coach. We keep a good pace and can run even longer or he takes his scooter to ride after me. It has become a pleasant weekly activity for him, my sister, and me. We're planning some family runs this summer. Seeds planted for me and him.

Everyone's closet now has a lot of running gear, and at family dinners we talk about our group goal and the kilometers we completed. We've decided to all go on a big memorable camping trip. You don't get tomorrow as a guarantee; you only get today. Live today like it's your last one. How would you live it differently? Lean into every opportunity you get. Now, I'm no longer asking for happy moments—I'm creating my own calm, happy times. I see everything differently. I'm ready to see the beauty in every moment. Thank you, intuition.

As I was lying in that bath, amazing ideas kept coming in. I asked my intuition: "Am I done my bath?" I felt the answer: "Nope, you'll know when you know." I'm not sure how long I was in there with my thoughts, but when my sister called, I understood I was ready to get out. She began the call by talking to me about her intuitive journey. And it is exactly what she needed.

We drove to a friend's house yesterday and continued our insightful conversation. We've been such close sisters for so long, and our talks are starting to reach new depths.

I had no set intention for a topic when we began. It just flowed, and I gave her real information. She cried and released. She wasn't crying out of sadness, she said, but because she felt my advice was a gift I was giving her. That is exactly how intuition works. I knew I was giving her information that she needed to hear and that she could handle. I told her I figured it out in my bath. I know I'm meant to hold the space for when someone is going through something. I'm holding space for a couple of people.

"Of course—I'm intuitive," my sister said. This was a eureka moment that she'd been experiencing. She'd been feeling it more often. She brought up our discussion to travel to Calgary, but both of us felt this intuitive stop. We both felt a block, like there was a reason we weren't supposed to go there this year. We decided to wait until we figured it out. Instead we felt we were meant to plan our upcoming multifamily camping trip, so that is where we decided to put our focus.

She stated that it was easier to see when something didn't fit. She said it was like when kids are trying to put the square peg in the round hole. When something doesn't intuitively match, you know. Once you start listening to intuition, you know when you're trying to put a square into a circle. That's what it feels like. You now know when intuition is in flow. When something doesn't fit, you feel it and you stop forcing it. Intuition stops you until it's right. There is a release because it feels good to know when something actually clicks into place, when something fits.

I came home one day, started prepping dinner. My husband was picking up our youngest from daycare, and they were on their way home, just like every day. I was thinking, is this all there is? Is this how our lives were going to look? I was worried that I would have to rush home from work to make food, then drive to activities. At that moment, I needed to change my life because I needed to slow down. When I unpacked where all this fear was coming from, it was the fear of missing out on my life and the people in it. I wanted to be there for pickup and drop-off at school, to enjoy the time with my family. I wanted to have dinner with my family. From there, I started to think about ways I could create that for myself and the people that I wanted to regularly connect with in my life. **The new perspective will come when you see that something can change. It depends on you.**

PLANT YOUR SEEDS

1. What is something you do to keep grounded on the noisiest day?

_____

_____

_____

_____

_____

_____

2. When is your personal teacup overflowing?

_____

_____

_____

_____

_____

3. What is something you want more of in your life?

_____

_____

_____

_____

4. How do you become the leader of your life?

_____

_____

_____

_____

_____

_____

_____

_____

5. Describe a memory you cherish with your family and/or friends.

_____

_____

_____

_____

_____

_____

_____

_____

_____

_____

_____

UNCOVERING YOUR PATH

IT'S ME

It's me sitting under this pink tree
The Alice of my own Wonderland
Taking the time to daydream
Living in a world in my head that slowly got created in front
of me
All champagne choices
All options I create for myself
With the guidance of the Universe, Source, Spirit, God
With the wind and delicate push forward under my feet
Forward, only ever forward
And the people you meet along the way
Give you just enough or the next key to move forward again.
They are a gift and what a gift to be me
I open the next box and learn something more about the true
me
I become even truer
Grounded in this true me.
It's special to realize what I thought was a daydream as a child
It was me foreshadowing and manifesting for my future
Knowing there is so much more
I forgot me for many years in between
Then my womb carrying a child woke me up
Released Her again.

Here I am daydreaming by my pink tree
With the warmth of the sun, wind on my face, and tears of
happiness pouring out
Yes, courage is what I have now
Courage to be
Just be and see
I now dance with myself and my ancestors
I can't help but feel their joy, pain, and excitement.
I am them and they are me
They've be waiting for me to see
To feel them supporting me
I feel you, all of you.

I am starting to feel the mighty silence. The silence that makes you smile because there is only good around you as there is joy in you. It is showing you the path to discovery. No matter what was going on in the world or in the home, my paternal Dido felt content. That is what I've been striving to achieve. To this day, I do not know who my Dido was, what he held dear, his inner thoughts. It is irrelevant because I know who he was in those silent moments, in the moments of nothingness. He was a man who made peace with the world and created joy. He created it for himself, and no one could take it away. No matter the chaos, sadness, hardship around him, he found his joy within himself. Now as I write this, I feel his silence. He showed me there is more strength in silence than in sound. He was not the type of person who told me to visit, but I know when I was there, we filled each other's emotional cups. A big part of our relationship was sitting or walking in complete silence.

Brother David Steindl-Rast says, "Stop, look, go." I couldn't do this before. Today, I slept in and woke up listening to the noises in my house. With my youngest in his crib, the sound of the heater, the silence. Three weeks ago, I woke up early and sat on my couch in silence. Appreciating the vast nothingness; it is big and unknown. I don't do it every day, but more and more frequently I appreciate what my grandfather was showing me. I think this was his greatest message. He lived in the present and lived everyday as if it were his last. He showed me that when I came to visit. His lesson was a long time in the making, but now I will keep discovering what he wanted me to see. I saw it in him, so I know it exists in me. For this lesson, I will be forever grateful and his peacefulness will live with me. I love the feeling that we are becoming one, even though we exist in different forms. What a gift he has left me! He planted those seeds for me. They are starting to grow.

I noticed how much I enjoy life when I look through my rose-colored glasses. Life looks so much better, and there is time to achieve everything. At this very moment, life is so pleasant because I create from within. I want to live a full life. I want my life to warm me up and give me purpose. This life keeps me on my path of self-discovery. We cannot prepare for everything that is to come, but we can go with the flow. Realize that it is not ours to control or change. This is the life of self-discovery, when you do not know what is in store, but you know that your intuition will provide you with the compass that you need. In this life, there are opportunities and experiences that present themselves to you, and you will act as you should when you follow your inner knowing. You cannot control the end results; it is out of your hands.

When I finished my master's, I had loads of expectations that I set for myself, which led to feeling like a victim in my situation. I had expectations around jobs, activities, return on investments, and business growth. So many expectations of when they would appear in my life. I didn't know then that gifts come when you are ready to fully receive them. That is what I noticed after all the personal development work. If I had received everything any earlier, I wouldn't know what to do with it all and where to go next.

For many years, I struggled with parts of myself, either my body, mind, or my overall self. I would then fall into a spiral of victim mentality, which was so hard to get out of. I would feel sorry for myself because no one else was doing that for me. That version of myself brought conflict and struggle to everything that I did. I would go to bed angry or bring anger, frustration, and disappointment to even simple everyday tasks.

I stood at the bottom of the stairs at our house and needed my husband to bring something. As I was calling for my husband with a sense of urgency to come help me, I looked over and saw my oldest mimicking me, hands on his hips, also calling for help. He must have been two. First of all, I thought to myself, I do not look that dramatic. Second, I did not want him taking on that behavior. That was a wake-up call, a pivoting moment when I decided I needed to change who I was showing up as at home. I didn't want that person being the role model. At the core, that is not who I am.

After working with coaches and finding out that the biggest gift you can give your child is your own happiness, I finally understood what I was doing wrong. I was putting myself in last place, and by the time I did have time for myself I was tired, uninspired, and only ready for the newest show on Netflix. When I decided to show up for myself, I changed the dynamic at home. My husband started focusing on himself, and my son saw me studying, learning, and practicing. He would ask, "Is this Pani so and so?" (Pani means Mrs. in Ukrainian and was the name of one of my coaches used by my oldest.) He even started recognizing their voices and would ask what I was learning about.

One day, I told him I was writing a book. He looked at me and pondered this new information. "Are there going to be pictures?" he asked. When I replied no, he added, "There needs to be pictures."

Hence the inspiration for my cover and section dividers. Later that day, he said he was also writing his book. He also paid attention to what my husband was doing. My oldest was at the top of the stairs ready to ask how many kilometers my husband ran every morning when my husband started running. Then every time we walked, went to the park, or biked, he wanted to know how many kilometers we did as a family. It was compelling being the observer to this change. We were all influencing each other.

When standing in the victim position, we think that the control for change is at the top and leads to the bottom. In reality, the control is at the bottom with all of us, only then can it move up the ladder. **We are where the change begins—we influence it from where we are.** The work starts with us and only when we know who we are in our reality do we start carrying that knowledge to our immediate family, our extended family and friends, our community, and beyond. From this place, we start showing up authentically to every conversation and interaction. People feel that authenticity, and only those who are on their journey will want to stay around to soak in your energy. Keep true to this feeling, it will make sure we all show up as our best selves. Our community will begin to emulate these parts of us that we are exploring and making space for. You will no longer be the victim, and instead you will become the changemaker. **It starts with you—you influence the energy that surrounds you.**

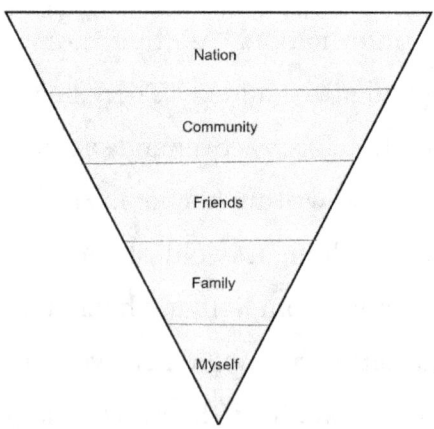

Our family dinner conversations changed when my husband started asking each of us, "What was your favorite part of the day?"

Now, my oldest starts these dinner conversations. It was done. I recognized how crucial this work was when my children were young because they were following our every move. Now my oldest even helps translate for my youngest about his favorite part of his day. My youngest is not talking yet, but he is still being understood.

When my youngest was born, I started working on myself. I hired personal development coaches, joined a mediation/conflict management program, started visualizations, gratitude, regular journaling, and found who I truly was at the core.

My conversations within my home used to come from a place of internal conflict. I was angrier when I wasn't working on myself. Now the conversations come from a calmer place, filled with gratitude, understanding, and compassion. I truly started listening and hearing what people were saying to me. I respect the day I have today and enjoy the moments it brings. It is so much easier being in a relationship with me because I am kinder to myself. This is the journey of life to keep evolving to our truest selves.

One evening, in a group coaching session, I started the session by asking everyone for an emotional check-in: "How are you today?"

Everyone shared how they were and something that kept coming up was that they didn't feel grounded. They felt like they were being pulled in so many directions. Everyone was sharing the same emotional state. Mid-session, I told them that I was holding space for them to be creative. I asked everyone to find paper and a pen or pencil and to sketch for twenty minutes using videos for inspiration and listening to music in the background.

By the end of the creative session, everyone created something that spoke to them. They came back to the group and were intrigued by their creativity. One woman shared a memory from when she was a little girl. Every time her family took a trip, her mom would buy a notebook for one way and another notebook for when they were going back home. In those notebooks, she would draw. When she had a moment for creativity she started remembering being a girl sitting on the train, hearing the tracks, and feeling the movement of the train. This activity brought back that childhood memory, and I thought to myself: "That's really all there is to it."

When we appreciate that there is playfulness that exists in all of us, we can create from a joyful place. I'm planting the seed for whoever needs it. By having these sessions, I am giving people a moment to breathe and find what they are looking for. They broke off into small groups and they discussed the ideas that came to them during the creative session. When they came back, everyone felt grounded. They came back to the group with different positive and radiating energy. They truly felt who they are in that moment, in their truest form.

Whenever I speak with friends or family, or run these group sessions, there is always a message for me too. I'm holding space for them and me. For my own self-worth. When we take ourselves to a whole other level, everyone benefits because they fill their cup with that energy. They then start moving to another level. I received positive feedback after that session, and one client told me how influential it was for her.

"Yes," I replied. "Because I've also started taking it to another level with myself." Coaching, mentoring, and positive relationships only work when we are doing the self-work. We then radiate warmth and growth from that genuine and kind place. You get comfortable sitting in the unknown, in the quiet of exploring. You change your life and as a by-product you change the lives of those around you. **You have to first create for yourself and then others will benefit. Always start with you!** Remember to ask yourself what you need at this time. There are people out there who also need it now. Share your journey. People are listening to your grounded creative self.

The seasons of your life are filled with change and newness that wasn't there before.

You keep doing your self-work and ground yourself in your values. The people that see your work are going to come in and want to be part of your growth. You will be inspired by this place. This includes your partner or spouse and your kids. You don't have to go and tip it into their mug. They'll know when they want in. That's the place to give from. Where you don't even have to go outside of yourself to give it. **You just have to be who you truly are, at your best loving, kind, compassionate self. You become love in its truest, purest sense.**

* * *

My mother-in-law saw me during my first mat leave reading and trying to understand infant behavior, sleeping, motherhood, eating, potty training . . . all possible topics. She immediately told me, "You should do something with this knowledge. You can help other mothers."

She was right, but at that moment, I didn't know what it could look like. What area of interest would I start with? How would I make this happen? I wasn't ready then because I still had much to learn about myself. Motherhood is a powerful gift, and not in the way I initially thought. It was truly a gift to me and to my future self, to crack open myself and see what really lies inside. I had to slow down and see the details.

PLANT YOUR SEEDS

1. If anything were possible and there were no limits to time, money, space, or opportunity, what would you want to be doing with your life?

_____

_____

_____

_____

2. When you think of what you want to leave behind, what is the first thing that comes to mind? Why this?

_____

_____

_____

3. Just like that the years go by. What is something you can do every day or week to move big ideas and goals forward? Where can you put it in your daily or weekly timeline so that it is getting accomplished?

_____

_____

_____

4. Write a letter to your child/children/niece/nephew/grandchild to read in the future (e.g., on a milestone birthday).

_____

_____

_____

_____

_____

_____

_____

_____

_____

_____

_____

_____

5. How do you see your journey?

_____

_____

_____

_____

_____

SECTION 3

REMEMBERING YOU ARE ALIVE

As life moves from our playful and childish ways, we forget the real reason we are here—to live a beautifully purposeful life. We forget that life is a gift worth treating with respect and focusing on above all else.

Use your time wisely! Focus on the goal and action it this year. The yearly seasons are a reminder of change and upcoming opportunity to reevaluate growth. Feel the purpose of the month before it begins by being present today.

I read Barack Obama's book *Dreams from My Father*, and he brought up a good point that has stayed with me. As he matured and as life events unfolded, he saw the importance of knowing where he was from and how it was a piece of him. This section highlights that your heart is connected to something bigger than you. You can even have your heart in a few places at once. You can be born and raised in one place and still be connected to this bigger pull elsewhere.

This is where generations can come together as you feel a part of this family story; the past, present, and future all come together. You start seeing your role or impact. You see your piece in this life puzzle. Respect your unique perspective and the story that comes with it. You've had the opportunity to know all your realities. You hold it all in your heart. You know that something ties you to land and place that you cannot define, it's bigger than you. When you feel this nudge or pull, it feels authentic and grabs you by the heart. This is the one life we are talking about. This one significant life you got gifted.

We all seek the place where you know who you are—that place is in us. The place of groundedness. Yes, it can be tied to language, culture, and traditions. It doesn't have to be tied to a country or borders. It is tied to intuition. The internal messaging. When you live life day by day, you have an opportunity to impact the next generation, not with words, but with that feeling. You were meant to be standing right here, right now. Not the one that's written in history books or defined by a culture or by others. You define it for the next generation. That's who this book is for.

EXPANSION

Feel is within
Your chest feels fuller
Your eyes see more
Your heart loves more and is grateful for less
Your arms embrace, everything
Let it expand
It feels like wind under your step
Blowing through your hair
Your energy is working and moving
In you, through you, from you
More goodness wants to come in
How could it not?
You are radiating, you are giving
You know how to receive all of this
Through your heart, through your love.

Our opportunity is to take the pieces of knowing and put them together, then define it in our own way. The beauty of the world is that we get to live in a world of other people's children. When I meet a man, who is in his fifties and has my son's name, I see more than just this man. I see my son being a fifty-year-old in this community. I see his abilities expand and his joy in the work he gets to do. When we all feel grounded and know who we are, we can lean into these directions, we find love for ourselves in this grounded life filled with empathy and understanding. We get better at sticking out a hand because we see our place in the story. **You are a piece of it all!**

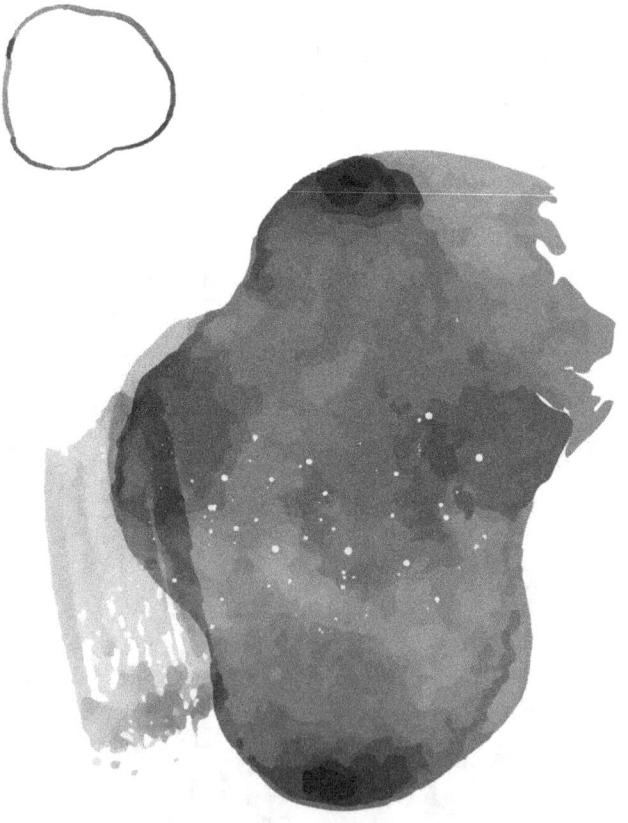

YOU ARE A PIECE OF IT ALL

I was on an airplane with my boys beside me, flying to Poland. They were finally both sleeping after a slow start to our journey. This was their first trip to Poland, where my parents, grandparents, and great-grandparents are from. Our extended family lives there. We always have a big family reunion when we return. My husband's family also lives in Poland; his parents moved to Canada in the mid-90s. The reason for the trip? My maternal grandmother's funeral. Maybe not the happiest occasion, but if you looked at the faces of my sons, all you can see is joy. The joy of meeting aunts, uncles, and cousins they have never met before. My oldest is getting to know where he is from, the meaning of this land to our family.

My five-year-old packed his whole bag and prepared for the trip in a couple of hours. He ran from room to room knowing what he was looking for to complete his mental packing checklist. We were talking on Tuesday; I told him his great-grandmother passed away and that we would be going to Poland. "Next year?" he asked.

"No, tomorrow" I replied. Immediately, the excitement could not be contained. Joy, even in these moments of change, we can experience the gift being given.

As we flew to Poland, I knew all of this learning and being was to get to this place. A couple of weeks earlier, I had a vision of my grand-mother. I get these in the middle of the day, while working, cooking, writing, etc. It doesn't matter, a vision comes to me when I am ready to know, when I am present in the activity. It means the Universe has a message for me. As a child, I would get these often, but I thought I was daydreaming. It was my intuitive hits all along. It's a message encouraging me to focus on this new piece of information. Sometimes it requires action, and sometimes I am expected to wait.

In my vision, I saw her soul was leaving her body. At that point she was still alive but slowly getting more ill. I knew her body would stay alive as long as we needed to get passports for the boys and our flights booked. Her spirit floated toward me with a lovely packaged gift. It was for me. She made it clear that her death was a gift to us. A gift to go there, to our family lands, and find what I have been looking for. I knew something was waiting, and it was for the next generation. The action I needed to take was clear.

After receiving passports for my boys, cinnamon hearts (because Valentine's Day was around the corner), and a yearly birthday photo album for my godson, I started packing these items. I started earlier because she was giving me the gift of time. Knowing it was coming and it was only a matter of time was a way of preparing everything for when the time came. The photo album arrived a week and a half earlier. I knew she would die in the next week. I kept asking my intuition if I had time to order items online. It became evident they would not come on time. She stayed alive long enough for me to figure out all of the last-minute details. All I had to do was book our flights: our gift.

Since the previous summer, my intuition kept nudging me to apply for the boys' passports. Finally, at the end of the year as the new year was around the corner, I knew I didn't have much time left. I went to get them done and then a couple of days later my aunt called to say that my grandmother was ill. I knew I needed to act fast to get the boys prepared for our journey.

She passed away on February 1, 2022. The call came from my aunt, everything was ready, and her body did not need to hold out any longer. I thought of my grandmother and said a special thank you for every gift she had given me before this point and everything she would still give me. In the last six months, I had bonded more and more with my grandmother without even talking to her or seeing her in person.

The next day—02.02.2022—was a day I had been planning since the beginning of the year. I knew it was going to be a significant day. I had planned a coaching event for that day because I wanted to be intentional. That was the day we would be flying. I thought those "2"s had to mean something powerful. And they did—that flight was unlike any I have taken. I knew this was exactly where I was meant to be, with my boys. Going directly to Warsaw. Even though my home has been in Canada, Poland has been the home for my soul. Bieszczady, our home for generations in the southeastern part of Poland, brings a warmth to my soul and overflows my heart with love.

As we landed in Warsaw, I was excited with butterflies. Knowing we were close to our destination.

Flying to Poland was a production when we were children. It required gifts for the whole family, tons of suitcases because you were able to have seventy pounds per suitcase, two per person. My sister and I would sit around the luggage, protecting everything, while my mom went to go figure something out. Once we were on the plane, we got to watch movies, read books, eat and drink, then fall asleep. My mom's sister and her husband were always ready to pick us up. They were always there and early. They put us and our oversized luggage into the car, then we were on our way. The drive to my grandparents, from Warsaw or Krakow, was long. My grandparents lived in a village in southeastern Poland. Always hours of driving, the road conditions were not what they are now. It was so long, and as a child it felt even longer; we would fall asleep and read some more. These trips would bring out my joy of reading, and I had so many books picked out to read. To this day, packing books for a trip is exciting and makes me smile. However, this time around I packed five notebooks because I knew I would be inspired to keep writing this book before the draft was due.

"Yak daleko? How far are we?" was the most popular question during these drives. We'd have to do pit stops and grab some food, sometimes we got to eat chips. I still buy chips at the airport in Poland and bring them home, especially as a treat for my sister. There is something about Polish chips; they fulfill the craving.

We would drive along the serpent roads through the mountains. We were getting to the end of our journey. I had a feeling take over of knowing we were close. Knowing we were close to my grandparents, to seeing them. I felt a feeling of true joy as we got closer and closer. I've regularly thought about my family in Poland. The things we didn't get to celebrate when we weren't together. For this reason, it was so exciting to see them and get together when we could. We all enjoyed it because it was rare. So I enjoyed it!

On the other hand, I remember the heaviness of the goodbyes. Ever since we were kids, my grandma would cry and say she didn't know when she would see us next. The goodbyes were layered. We'd get to the airport and do the same thing. When I think about airports, I remember our visits filled with joy and sadness. At the beginning of our journey, it was tears of gratitude that we're all together. Then at the other end, there were many tears, especially for my younger sister, when we left. It was the norm. Now when I go to the airport, not nearly as often, I love seeing people connect with their families. I love the meaningful hellos you get to see when two people who have truly missed each other reconnect. The thought of it brings tears to my eyes.

We were close. In Warsaw, we hopped onto the next airplane to get to Rzesow. Again, I felt the excited butterflies. My oldest was exhausted but kept on going with support and encouragement. My two-year-old did not get nearly enough sleep. With a quick nap on the second flight, we finally landed at our destination. With our car rental figured out, I knew the next feeling. How long until those hilly serpent roads? Until that green sign that showed we had reached our destination? This time it was closer, the trip was quicker. I guess between maturing and my self-work, the journey became more enjoyable. Or maybe the roads had improved?!

We got to our destination. There were the tired yet excited kids, the unpacking, the crunch of snow, the fresh air, the burning wood. I took it all in and thought to myself that it was the most charming place on Earth. We entered that house with smiles and hugs, and my grandmother's gift kept on giving. This was only day one, and there was still so much in this offering.

On Friday, we went to see her body in the funeral home. I knew she was now more in my heart than in this body. My oldest asked so many questions, and through his questions I was learning how I wanted to grieve this time around, not just follow traditions. How I wanted to remember the dead and the gifts they gave us. As we were singing songs at the funeral home, her spirit lives in all of us. She made all of us into strong and resilient human beings. People who kept their feet on the ground. She was the matriarch of our family. It was the end of a chapter in our family's earthly life. Her children stood around her body, tears flowing, and love in our hearts. The torch was passed.

I was standing and looking in the bathroom mirror at my tear-stained face, and I understood why I was here. My boys would get to say goodbye to their great-grandmother, meet their great-grandfather, who was dealing with dementia, and meet their paternal great-grandmother, my husband's grandmother. She was the last one who would have something to pass on to them, to their earthly lives. We were going to see her the next week.

Saturday was the funeral.

We arrived a bit later with the kids so that they could handle the long day. When we got there all was good, and the sermon started. My aunt wrote a summary of her mother's life. The priest was about to begin and read her letter, when my youngest pulled on my jacket to go to the bathroom. There wasn't a bathroom in this old church, so we went to the car so he could use the potty. Back we came to hear some more when my oldest now needed to use the toilet. I laughed to myself. We figured it out, and I wasn't meant to hear my aunt's words from the priest anyway. I would ask my aunt to personally share the message.

We walked from the church up the snowy, icy path to her grave site as a family. The kids, grandkids, and great-grandkids. My cousins and I were bigger now. We took up more space, and our family had expanded. I had not seen everyone for over seven years, and we had all changed. The family said their final goodbyes with the last ounces of tears streaming down our faces. We stood together, and I felt such gratitude to be there with everyone at this moment. My youngest wanted me to hold him the whole time we were outside. My arms were getting tired, but my heart was full. *Thank you, Baba, for all you have given to us. We will be forever grateful.* As they lowered the coffin, I knew this was the end.

Walking into the hall for the wake, I felt so much positive energy radiating from those who attended. So many people were gifting my grandmother and her family love. We were sitting together and reminiscing about her. There was a slideshow of her life with so many pictures of her and my grandfather. I even saw a YouTube video of them touring a group of tourists around their birthplace, Yavirnyk. They each lost their memories and their abilities, but they never lost hold of each other. They were a constant in each other's life.

That day, I set the intention to speak with fewer people but to have more meaningful conversations. I received so much learning from wonderful people. People who found themselves and figured out how they wanted to lead their lives. They built a life that they manifested. They lived from that place of feeling, which was exactly what I had been learning over the last two years. My conversations all left me with a fullness. At the end of the night, I spoke with everyone who I needed to speak with.

The next day we went to my aunt's. As my sons watched *Cars* (in Polish) with their cousins, she read me the letter she wrote about her mother. Here is the letter about my grandmother's life, written by her daughter, for her funeral, and translated by me:

Deceased Olha was born, the second daughter of Anna and Theodore Palynsky, on April 21, 1937, in Yavirnyk (Jawornik), the week before Easter, on Palm Sunday. She was born prematurely in the seventh month. Olha was a weak infant so both of her grandmothers realistically evaluated the situation. They did not think she had a chance to survive. Her mother, Anna, after a difficult labor, did not have breastmilk or the strength to take care of the infant. Her grandmother fed a small little Olha with cow's milk that was given to her in drops that dripped from a clean cloth. They carried her to a neighbor's house, where a woman who had small children would feed Olha with her milk. The baby girl continued to grow and gain strength with each day.

At the beginning of the 1940s, Olha's father, Theodore, was sent to Germany for forced labor. Anna followed after him, leaving the two little girls to be cared for by the grandmothers. The girls were split up. Maria, the older sister, stayed in Yavirnyk, and Olha was sent to Turzansk (Turynske in Ukrainian) with the other grandmother. This was the happiest period in her life. Olha always remembered her time with her cousin, Andrij, playing by the river, her caring babusia (grandmother), uncle and his wife. In 1946, history changed their fate forever. Her beloved grandmother was deported to Soviet Ukraine. They never saw each other again.

A year later, with her parents, Olha was forcibly resettled during Operation Vistula to regained territories close to Kolobrzeg. This is where she experienced her adolescent and early adult years. Every day she worked long and hard on the fields with her parents. She found time to participate in religious and community activities that were organized by the resettled Ukrainians. She participated in Sunday mass 80 kilometers away. This is where she met Ivan, who told her about his first memories with his father in their faraway mountains.

Olha and Ivan married in 1964. A year later, they had their first daughter, Hania (my mother). The young couple decided to return to their lands with a three-month-old. They took an unchristened Hania because they wanted her to be christened in their hometown in the Karpaty. They moved to Rzepedz (Reped in Ukrainian), where they built their home and had three more children: Darek, Eva, and Mirosia.

This was a difficult time in Olha's life. Everyday responsibilities were above and beyond her strength, but she never gave up and kept going. She was hardworking and full heartedly engaged in her responsibilities. Occasionally, she was surprised that no one in the family could keep up with her. Her strength was unmatched. Olha helped her daughter, who was born deaf, receive therapy. She raised her children to be people who could figure out life on their own. She did not judge her children's choices and rarely criticized their ways. She had pride in their achievements and valued their accomplishments. Olha was happy when her kids traveled and got to see the world. For her family, she put aside her own wishes.

Olha lovingly lived with her husband for fifty-seven years. Their long and healthy lives allowed them to enjoy being with their grandchildren. She got to meet eleven grand-children and four great-grandchildren; almost all of them made it to her funeral for the final goodbye.

Even today, the weather symbolizes her life, which was filled with sacrifice and hardship achieved through exhaustive work.

In eternal memory.

I sat at their kitchen table hearing these words for the first time—I hadn't known all of the details of her story. I remembered her hard-working and continuous momentum and that no one could keep up with her. Her strength and resilience lives in all of us every day. That is yet another gift she left with us.

How would you live your life differently if you lived today like it was your last? What would you start noticing? Today would definitely have a different meaning, and we wouldn't be in such a rush to move into the next day. You would appreciate the role you play in this intergenerational puzzle. There would be an impact in everything that you do.

PLANT YOUR SEEDS

1. As you look at your ancestral history, who are you? What resonates with you?

_____

_____

_____

_____

_____

2. What experiences do you remember about your family?

_____

_____

_____

_____

_____

3. When you think about family, what feelings and memories
   come up for you?

_____

_____

_____

_____

_____

4. How do these experiences make you feel?

_____

_____

_____

_____

_____

_____

_____

_____

5. Where do you and your abilities fall into your family story? List and describe more than one.

_____

_____

_____

_____

_____

_____

_____

_____

_____

_____

THE MAGIC OF YOU

Your story
Share it, tell it, explore it.
We want to know, we want to listen
This is how we connect, we make space.
You make it easier for me through you
You have so much to offer
Share it, tell it, explore it.
It gives us a place of sameness
Your talents, abilities, experiences
We want to talk about it.
You draw us in
Share it, tell it, explore it.
You have an aura
It draws us in
Makes us want to know
More, more, more.
Your path is worth sharing
We are all connected. Your story is mine too.
When you help one person, you help all those around
Share it, tell it, explore it.
We've known our truths for a long time
We forgot about them for a period of time because of life.
There comes a moment where we again remember who we are
And why we are here
We know our purpose and that is when we soar
When we heal ourselves and those around us
We share our gifts
Share it, tell it, explore it.

YOU ARE HERE TODAY

Prior to writing this book, prior to becoming a mother, prior to doing the self-work and learning, I was compassless. I did not feel like I had a clear direction. I didn't know what my talents were supposed to be used for. That feeling of being without a compass was indifference. Indifference would be the end of my family story if I didn't do something with my life. All these valuable items are right in front of us; we all have familial and cultural pieces that we hide in a drawer or sell off because they don't match our style or decor. All of these pieces are our familial artifacts and are meant to be seen, but we are indifferent to keeping or showing them. There are also the spiritual artifacts that live in all of us, even as we become the next generation. They are a part of us.

Working with my intuition and leaning in to my ancestral stories connected me back to my responsibility. What is "the more" to life that so many of us are searching for? A necklace from my father's village was sitting in my drawer waiting for me to wake up intuitively and see that it was part of me. It was me who shares the story and makes the connections. It would not be done for me or my family; it would only be done through me. I used to go through the motions of the day, but now, since becoming a mother, I stop to see and to enjoy. At a recent gathering, I saw this firsthand. I went to the event and appreciated the details, the notebooks, the snacks, the decor, and more importantly, I actually listened to what people were saying.

In the past, I was passionate about so many things but not with a sense of purpose and responsibility. Now, with every new day I get gifted, I know it is on me to add value, to share. Let it in! Share it. Let it flow through me and around me. Let those intuitive nudges come in because there is more to this life. The energy wants an invite, so I invite it in. I am available to hear more, to embrace it all. I am ready!

"THE OPPOSITE OF LOVE IS NOT HATE, IT'S INDIFFERENCE. THE OPPOSITE OF ART IS NOT UGLINESS, IT'S INDIFFERENCE. THE OPPOSITE OF FAITH IS NOT HERESY, IT'S INDIFFERENCE. AND THE OPPOSITE OF LIFE IS NOT DEATH, IT'S INDIFFERENCE."

—Elie Wiesel

As I was listening to Oprah's Super Soul Sunday conversation with Elie Wiesel, I froze when I heard him share this quote on indifference. At that moment, as I was preparing breakfast and doing my morning routine, I realized that for most of my life I was indifferent to my culture, to my heritage, to my language, to our land. Yes, it always had meaning to me. Yes, I learned the language and read to my children. Yes, I sent them to a Ukrainian daycare. I heard my grandparents' stories about hardship maintaining their culture, religion, and language in a time and place in history where it was not allowed. However, at the end of the day, so many cultural "artifacts" were sitting in my drawers unloved and unappreciated. There was a necklace from my father's village, purchased from a woman who was an expert in patterns, colors, and regional history. It represented women's passion, pain, beauty, womanhood, hardship, and storytelling. The way women shared their creativity. I heard Elie's message loud and clear. I would not put the story away in the back of my mind, like I put the necklace in the back of my jewelry box.

Indifference. Indifference. Indifference. It rang in my ears, in my mind, in my heart for months after hearing the podcast. That message was for me. Indifference happens when we think someone else is responsible for the destiny, the decision, the outcome. When really all along we are the ones responsible. I am responsible for what I feel, what I hold dear, and what I share with others and my community. Melt away the indifference, and under all those layers, you'll find your purpose. The reason you are here and what it truly means to you, without the labels and expectations. What do you want? What do you really want out of this one life that is given to you?

I live a life of security and regularity. I never felt the need to fight for it in the way my grandparents did, the way previous generations did. As I stood in my kitchen that morning with these raw feelings of responsibility, I wondered what I should do next. *How do I make my actions and my love make a difference? How do I make a difference?* My intuition has shown me.

There is the story of Dido and the first memory of his dementia, where he approached me to discuss some of the things he didn't like, specifically about the way our family did things. We were in my cousin's room, in Poland. He started sharing all of these judgments that he had. The way my mother raised us to the way that my mother did things. It was a version of my grandfather I'd never seen. He was so angry. He was erratic, irrational. He did not come from a place of joy, gratitude, and kindness. He came from this place of anger. I was in absolute shock. And I thought to myself, how could he hate everything about my family this much? It didn't make sense.

I don't know if this conversation was five or thirty minutes long. For me, it felt long, irrational, like an out-of-body experience. I remember leaving that room and feeling like I needed to get out. I locked myself in the bathroom and cried. I was so angry with him that he wasn't his usual loving self.

At that moment, I did not have empathy or understanding. At that time, we didn't know that he was sick. I later came home to Canada and shared the story with my parents. They told me that no one would ever love your way of life and that it's not on me. After a few years, we found out he was going through dementia. Reflecting back, we suspect that outburst was the first sign.

It was such an ugly memory I had with my grandfather that doesn't match any other memory I've had with him. After we received his diagnosis, I was so grateful that it could be "blamed" on dementia because I could build empathy. I started treating my grandfather differently, and I could protect all the previous memories I had of him.

It's eye-opening when you have an experience with someone that is different from every previous experience. From that point on, our relationship wouldn't be what it was. And in that moment, I grieved my grandfather. I grieved for the version of him I would never see again. And because I went to Poland less and less frequently, the dementia was getting worse and worse. I keep all those warm memories of him, all his stories, his delightful way of looking at life, his poems, and the things he would talk about alive in my heart and my mind.

I didn't get to see him every day, and as a child, I would struggle with the limited in-person contact. Being the child of immigrant parents, the immigrant story breaks up the story of family because all of the family traditions and the family stories are disconnected. Your parents moved away from all their cultural norms, their community. It's one generation that changes reality. I grew up seeing my grandparents every two years, occasionally more often if they visited, which was not that frequent. Our relationship was different from the relationship they had with my cousins who lived in Poland.

Now, as I have my own sons, our traditions are different and they're going to change from what even my parents upheld because they kept traditions from home. We are going to make new traditions. My boys' exposure to our culture and heritage is going to be different from mine because our immediate family lives in Canada. I'm starting to feel this shake-up in my identity, of what I will show them, what I want them to see, and what they will one day continue with their families.

I asked my oldest about attending Ukrainian Saturday School and Ukrainian dancing, both of which he dismissed. "No, I'm not interested. I'd rather be at home with you. But I'd love to play baseball."

I'm realizing his sense of reality is different from my own. He has two English-speaking parents whose identity is Canadian, while I had two parents whose identity was very much Ukrainian-Polish-Eastern-European and Canadian. He doesn't see that in me; he doesn't see that in us.

Our parents showed us love for our culture through all of this, and as the years go on, will my boys see that for themselves? What does this generation do with my grandparents' story, with my grandparents' experiences of protecting who they are and their identity? Where does that leave the rest of us?

I feel like I'm in the center of it all. **I'm in the center of the past, the present, and the future.** We have it good because things are going well; we could be whoever we want to be. I don't have to hold on so tight. My grandparents had to hold on tight to their identity. How do I add to their story? When will I weave myself in?

These intuitive nudges keep moving in me. They keep me focused, pausing, and taking the time to listen. They are showing me when to be. November was a writing month, but I wasn't supposed to write more because I was missing something. I still needed to uncover more. I knew that as December rolled around something would present itself and those words would be put on paper.

I watched the movie *Encanto*, and as the main character Maribel explores her internal magic, certain pieces became more clear. I saw myself in the main character. I—through various generational experiences and trauma—exist. It is once I start caring and stop being indifferent that I will acknowledge my role. My place. When I will hear it in the voice from within. When do I become a part of the narrative and the main character of my own story? I used to tell myself, these were responsibilities of those who were bigger than me. But if not me, then who?

I've created a sacred space for myself filled with feel-good items. I have lemongrass and sage, and I also have my Ukrainian embroidered handkerchief, nesting dolls, a beaded necklace, a hand-painted Highbush Cranberry "kalyna" jewelry box—they are all on display.

After my grandmother's funeral, we all "inherited" a few items, and I couldn't help but take her handkerchiefs. Baba used them when she was working the field. As my son regularly talks about us owning this farm, I'll need these. Is that why I took them?

"LEARN WELL, THINK, READ; LEARN WHAT IS
FOREIGN TO YOU BUT DO NOT FORSAKE YOUR
OWN. FOR THOSE WHO FORGET WHAT THEIR
MOTHER TAUGHT THEM WILL ANSWER TO
GOD."

—Taras Shevchenko

Growing up and spending our summer vacations in Poland, I often heard my maternal grandfather recite a poem by Shevchenko to us. He was a lover of Ukraine, Ukrainian culture, and a supporter of independence from the former USSR. He was constantly reading and sharing his findings with everyone at home. I remember him reading with his glasses on and taking the time to tell me what he was consuming. I love those memories I have of him. The love for his land, faith, and culture poured out of him.

My maternal grandparents lived in a small village in the southeastern corner in the Subcarpathian Mountains, Yavirnyk (now Jawornik). Post-WWI, this borderland culture was a part of Poland; however, their culture, religion, and language were tied to Ukraine. This area held meaning to the people who lived there, and it continues to hold space in the next generations' hearts. It is where we go to remember previous generations and their struggles. We walked by my grandfather's childhood home, which is currently rubble in tall grass and their apple tree. Now, it is a beautiful forest with a chapel, where there once was a church and cemetery. No one lives there, but we still remember.

Many years ago, they had received a warning that they would be removed from their homes and relocated to a different area. They had to pack up their valuables. Just like that a village was emptied and their lives left behind. Children were holding on to their parents, who looked ahead and kept moving forward. Their wagons were packed and their animals led forward. They were loaded onto trains and moved to the north of Poland. The homes they moved into were the homes of Germans who had been deported back to Germany after the war. It was a place they never knew, but that they now were to call home.

In this process of longing, they deepened the love for their land. They planted seeds of love for Ukraine and Ukrainian culture in the next generations. We may be dispersed all over the world, but our love has not diminished.

Seventeen years later, my grandparents got married. My grandmother was twenty-seven and my grandfather was thirty-five. They had my mother. Finally, they were able to go back and start a new life on their ancestral lands. This is how my grandparents would tell us about their life. This was their story. Never published but always shared.

Since I was a child, their stories have been etched into my mind and heart. Often as a mother, I think about the hardship of leaving a place you love for uncertainty. The fear of people forcing your relocation. I have seen my privilege from a young age. That I was never forced out. Only in university did I understand that my privilege was deeper than I initially thought. Not only was I never forced to relocate, I also never had to immigrate and start again. I remember as a child my mother and father being corrected when they spoke English and not with kindness. I saw their immigration as a part of me. However, in university, I was asked what private school I went to—I would never be seen as a child of immigrant parents or of grandparents who struggled to come back to their lands. I never had to fight for who I am. I was detached from that reality. I did not emulate hardship, I emulated privilege. From this place, I write this book. From complete gratitude to my parents, grandparents, and all my ancestors who showed us the beauty of our ancestral land, the pride of our story, and the beauty of our culture and dialect.

I'm not my parents' story. No one can see that I'm the oldest child of immigrant parents. Everyone sees that I speak English the way that I do. In various situations that I'm in, I am seen as privileged. I'm a person who has doors wide open. At the same time, I went to work and was talking to colleagues about the holidays and taking some time off for Christmas, which we celebrate on January 7, as we follow the Julian calendar. They looked at me and said, "Really? You're not that religious."

In that moment, it is very easy to be indifferent as the next generation. I try to keep in mind that I represent something bigger in that moment. I heard my grandparents tell me all the things they've had to fight for to have their language, culture, and lands. To be able to celebrate what they celebrate. I understood my responsibility, but at the same time, I thought it was so easy to just conform. I think about my grandparents often, especially as their memories of their past faded and they were no longer able to understand their present life. It is easy for me to fit in and continue living a very comfortable life. I keep those things top of mind after having children. They showed me the importance of talking about these ancestral details, and that I'm the key to the future because we are all a piece of the puzzle.

I hear them, I am conscious of them. I will try to teach love to these cultural aspects. See how the next generation could see this in a different context while still fight for the same message. I see my responsibility. The gatherings women had in the village, they were having masterminds this whole time. We have always wanted to gather and share ideas. It was not meant to be a lonesome endeavor.

The diaspora understands that you are holding onto a lot of identity pieces, specifically language. That is why my siblings and I went to Ukrainian Saturday school. To learn about Ukraine, the history, literature, culture, and geography. In Eastern Europe, they used to have a lot of oral examinations, which were used in our Saturday school. For grade 11, we had to complete exams for all four courses in front of our classmates and a panel of teachers. To this day, thinking about these exams and my piano exams with the Royal Conservatory of Music, makes my hands sweat. One of the questions was to recite a few lines of a famous poem. I recited it well but introduced it incorrectly. I was trying to recite the poem by the famous Ukrainian poet Taras Shevchenko. My grandfather would be proud that out of the many things he showed me, this rings in my ears and heart.

My father often vouched for us as kids. When we were supposed to be cleaning on a Saturday but were dragging our feet, he would say to my mother: "Life will teach them." My parents gave us a lot and then some. They would say education is priority number one. There were no exceptions. Everything was taken care of for us so that we could learn. When my husband and I had our boys we knew that the baptism gifts would be put into their education fund. These are generations of parents giving their kids more than they gave themselves. Passing the torch. We can do the same and keep our emotional cups full.

My paternal grandparents never were relocated because their fathers worked for the railway. They were already at the station to relocate, but they were turned around. They were seen as essential workers for their communities. Their land was still theirs. Over time my grandparents bought land in the '60s to build their own home for their two kids and their youngest who was about to be born, my father. My father and cousins inherited this land after my grandfather's death. As we were sitting together on my last visit and discussing the projects, I thought how pleasant it is to hear about the multigenerational projects that will keep being created. The creativity of generations is coming together and giving this precious land meaning.

My family held onto a lot of fear. Fear from a place of loss of who they were and also what they saw that I was never a witness to. My husband is half-Polish and half-Ukrainian. His parents are also immigrants from Poland who came to Canada when he was five years old. I went to Poland alone after we started dating and told my paternal grandfather about my then boyfriend and his family. Immediately, I saw the sadness in him. It was in his body language, since he was a man of few words. I knew he felt sad because my husband was half-Polish. I never judged my grandfather for this because he lived in a world I will never fully comprehend. He saw things, I cannot even imagine. He saw hate in a way I did not.

After a few years of dating, we vacationed in Poland and met each other's families. We visited my grandfather together. Then on one of our last days, we went to say goodbye. He hugged us so hard, as if sending us all the love that he had. We walked down the path from his house and he stayed behind. I could see the love and joy he had for us. As I looked back, I knew we had a blessing even though that wasn't what we came for. It was exactly what I needed to feel. A memory that will stay with me forever because it was the last time I saw him alive. I cried as we continued down the path and over the river across the bridge.

We had a filling Thanksgiving dinner at our aunt's and as we were eating dessert, we started talking about identity. Who do we feel we are? What is our identity? Who are you? We all had a different idea and understanding of what that meant to us. That night I heard two impressive messages. As I regularly say now, "Yes, I hear you, Universe." The challenge is that you feel that you are neither here nor there, which is a hard place to live. It is easier when you understand that you get to live being both. Wow, that was exactly what I needed to hear! The other message, from my father-in-law, was that he never felt the same connection to land that my family felt because his family was deported at the same time as my grandparents and was always preparing to be deported again, even though it did not happen again. They never felt rooted where they were. I felt a moment of privilege. How fortunate I was in being able to accept the meaning of land and its role in my family.

A few weeks prior to this outing, I chatted with a friend. We discussed how when you go back to Poland, they call you "Kanadolki" (girls from Canada). She said, "It sounds like a swear word."

I thought about it and responded, "It is in a way, but I now take it as a compliment." As a child when they said it to you, it meant: you were privileged; you didn't grow up the way they did; you didn't understand them or their way of life. You didn't know the things they did. I was Canadian and Ukrainian. As I grew up and discovered where I felt rooted, I knew I was actually Canadian with a tie to the land my ancestors were from and the dialect they spoke. The dialect is a mix of Ukrainian and Polish because they lived in mixed-language communities. The land is in Poland. For me this sliver of land is exactly where I need to be.

On the same trip, with my husband, I visited his mom's family. They have a big family, and we went there for his cousin's wedding. What a welcome we got! Everyone was inviting and wanted to learn about me and my interests. My husband's maternal grandparents live in a multigenerational home you never want to leave. The warmth and love can be felt immediately. Just like that I was not only accepted but loved. I then chatted with his grandmother, who is Polish, about the relationship they had with the Ukrainians in their community. The churches were side-by-side, and no one worked on the other's holidays. Everyone respected each other and celebrated family milestones together. She then started singing a Ukrainian song and my eyes watered. I knew I wanted to be a part of this family. I met his grandfather and saw what my husband's face would look like in his 80s. Now when I look at my oldest son, I see both of them in his face.

To this day, there are things that will always put a smile on my face like polka music, the accordion, the double bass, embroidery, and the winding road to my grandparents. My parents participated in Ukrainian dance, and my husband and I did as well. We're also teaching our boys the love of Ukrainian dancing, and we hope these elements of love keep being passed down.

On our last trip for my grandmother's funeral, I saw something come through, especially for my oldest. He learned who he is in the world. He is all of these things. For me, I could be all of these things and at the same time none of these things. I get to choose, and I do not have to accept all of these labels. **I just am.**

My grandparents lived in their boldness, my parents lived in their boldness. Now it is my turn so I can then show that to my children. The power within me. It's about being a part of our ancestors and leaders for the next generations. We all have a role. We all play a part in our family history. I am currently discovering mine. I am sharing this part of my story because **once we all share our ancestral stories with ourselves, others, and the future generations,**

we draw the picture of the world and the beauty of who we all are. These are the stories that are worth sharing because in the end we are all part of the same puzzle.

I have grown. I expanded my mind and explored what my full potential really is. I have leaned into intuition, curiosity, and creativity. I have learned more about myself in one year than I have in my entire life. In this process of uncovering, many monumental experiences were with my past self, all the firsts. I had the joy of learning from those experiences.

The connection we have to our ancestors lives in all of us. This idea hit me when I was reading Barack Obama's book *Dreams from My Father*, where he is in search of who he is on his paternal side in Kenya. After meeting his granny and aunt for the first time, he reflects:

"IT WASN'T SIMPLY JOY THAT I FELT IN EACH OF THESE MOMENTS. RATHER, IT WAS A SENSE THAT EVERYTHING I WAS DOING, EVERY TOUCH AND BREATHE AND WORD, CARRIED THE FULL WEIGHT OF MY LIFE; THAT A CIRCLE WAS BEGINNING TO CLOSE, SO THAT I MIGHT FINALLY RECOGNIZE MYSELF AS I WAS, HERE, NOW, IN ONE PLACE."

–Barack Obama

I've been lucky enough to have parents who went with us to Poland every second summer when we were young. I got to learn about where we came from and what life used to look like for the people in these communities. With that, I've learned a lot about where my great-grandparents used to live and the realities of their life. It's a village that no longer exists, Yavirnyk. The next generations, with my grandparents, parents, aunts, uncles, cousins, and siblings, hike there. My maternal grandparents spoke of the love for their lands and nature, which was shown during these treks. As a child, I may not have grasped the importance of what they were saying, but now I see they were showing gratitude. They moved back to the closest village possible to their nonexistent community. After they got married, they could not see themselves living anywhere else.

As we hiked, the grass was tall and the trek always felt long, but when we reached the spot, all you could see was happiness and connection. There's a cemetery there now. We would say our prayers and thank the previous generations for their commitments. We crossed ourselves in front of the restored chapel. It led to multigenerational bonfires, sausages charred by the fire, and singing. Always singing.

Now that I look at it, maybe this was our way of respecting and showing gratitude to those generations before us. It was energetically tied to something bigger. We would walk by my grandparents' home and where they were born. Their homes no longer exist, but the apple tree was still on my grandfather's childhood property. My maternal grandfather loved sharing his stories. We have heard so many childhood stories through these hikes. This connection to ancestry is a big part of true gratitude. Gratitude for knowing how you got here, being rooted in who you are, and who you want to be. It helps to keep you true to yourself and to your values.

Going to Poland is my most popular summer memory. I feel like all my summer adventures and memories were created in Poland. As children, that is where we spent the majority of our summers. It was what I thought summers were, going to your grandparents' village and hanging out on their farm, while getting to pick delicious fruits and vegetables straight from the vine or the bush.

My paternal grandfather had joyful living figured out. Every day he went on a long walk in nature, in the hills that he loved, in silence. Whenever I got to join him, we barely talked, and I loved it. He was different from everyone else because he seemed most content with himself and his own thoughts. I was grateful when I got to join in. Again we barely talked, but I felt connected on a personal level. However, one of his stories that I do remember is the one about his WWII wound. A bullet grazed his upper arm. When I heard this story, I remember thinking how close it was to us not existing. My father. Us. We all wouldn't exist. I find that this memory comes to me often in my everyday life, and it is where the core of my gratitude comes from. I do not know all of the struggles of my ancestors or all of their stories of near-death experiences, but I know that his story was not the only one. It brings me closer to my ideas around opportunity. That because of his life I get to live a life filled with opportunities, and it is

I who needs to lean into these ideas. I have opportunities because of previous generations' struggles. **There is opportunity in having the ability to live. We get to exist and we get to create.** I'm very honored and hope that with every opportunity I create something of value.

My paternal grandfather, Dido, died in the fall of 2011. When he passed away, I learned a lot about my cultural and familial way of mourning. He was the first closest family member who passed away when I was an adult. It was about having an appropriate amount of time to mourn depending on your relationship to someone. A spouse, child, or parent is one year; a sibling is six months; and a grandparent is three months. You are supposed to wear dark colors during this time, and there is to be no dancing or overly joyful activities. He lived for eight-five years. I gave him a year of daily thinking about him, even if it was for five minutes. I thought about him every night and conversed with him. Sometimes I cried, sometimes I laughed, but every night it was a deliberate connection.

In my journal entry, on Friday January 27, 2012, I wrote that his death was supposed to teach me a few things:

- You never have anything forever, so do it now.
- How to mourn someone with respect and love, and to think about them every day.
- For me to fly to his funeral and meet family I had never met before. To make time to honor someone. I was able to leave for two weeks while in university, and it was easier than I thought.

- For him to inspire something in me.
- For me to learn something from the people who are here and now.
- He is closer to me spiritually than in his human form.
- For me to have the first one-on-one trip with my dad and get a chance to bond differently.
- Be more spiritually connected to something bigger than me and my life.

Komancza (Kom-an-cha) is the village where my father was born and raised. He lived there until he moved to Canada in 1989. It is a charmingly simple place. When I go there, I am surrounded by generations of family who live—and lived—there. We have our usual route going to visit my dad's sister, then his brother. We slowly get to my cousin's house who lives in the family home. There is a barn on the property, which is getting redone into a summer home. Eventually, we get to the cemetery and light a candle for my grandparents and great-grandparents. Everyone gets seen and remembered. In Eastern Europe, as in many cultures, the dead are not any less important than the living. They also receive respect and remembrance. Isn't that beautiful?

As a teen, I remember going to a local woman who created traditional paintings, icons, and necklaces from the area. Listening to her passion to put this together was impressive to my young ears as

I started to learn more and more about the history of the area and the people who lived there. I have always been drawn to the past and the future, and the connectivity of both of those to our life story. It is only recently that I truly started enjoying the present. One of the items I purchased from her was a traditional beaded necklace in the local colors and style. It was my gift from the past. I wore it for the first time many years later for a recent Christmas photoshoot for my website and social media. I got a hit from intuition to put the focus on embroidery, and I knew this was the right place to wear it.

I knew it was for "them" in the past. It was me paying respect to those who were and continue to be in the next generations. I felt connected like we were all one. The photos show me and I feel them. My eyes water as I think about the beauty of that day and the gift of creativity they passed on. Embroidery is a big part of our creative journey. It did not end with them; it continues to be used in modern ways. Every Christmas and Easter we take out the embroidery we have received from family or as gifts. It is that remembrance of the past. It will keep being passed down with love for special occasions and celebrations. That day celebrating my intuitive coaching business, I saw their role in every milestone I experienced and knew that they are never far away.

One morning, I woke up at 4:40 a.m., after a long break from my 4:30 wake-ups when my boys were babies. There was an intensity to those early morning hours. I prepped breakfast for the boys, then sat down to my favorite visualization song. My eyes were wide open and it flowed in. With such vividness, it brought tears to my eyes. Happy, joyful tears are becoming the norm.

When I wake up this early in the morning, especially when it is dark and cold, I think about my maternal grandparents, who were farmers with early wake-up times. I imagine them getting ready to feed the animals. I feel connected to the past them, in the present moment. That we are living parallel morning routines. I feel connected to something bigger than me and my situation at that time of day. I feel their youth and the wisdom they uncovered during their lives. It is a life filled with purpose, love, and care.

During those summers in Poland, I remember waking up to chicken being prepared for chicken noodle soup. They had a lot of chickens and every once in a while one got picked for dinner. My grandparents would be preparing the meat with joy and care, chatting away. I loved seeing them doing their farm and garden work. I would either join them or watch from a distance. Their bond was evident when they went to pick red currants or gooseberries. They would sit on their small stools and chat. They were always chatting about something! With all the love they put into the soup, it always tasted delicious. My grandmother was great at a lot of things, but domestic work was not a part of her favorites. Nevertheless, I loved her chicken noodle soup. This is why at my wedding, the soup we served was chicken noodle soup.

My father makes food every Sunday from breakfast to dinner. It was either a sausage with veggies or an omelet with veggies. Then for dinner, a giant pot of chicken noodle soup that would cook for hours, with egg noodles or potatoes or both. Both is my favorite option. You eat it like a meal. To this day, Sunday brunch is a must at my parents.

My mother-in-law also prepares chicken noodle soup on Sundays. In the morning, she would prepare delicious sandwiches for breakfast, and soup cooking for hours meant the beginning of dinner. Whenever I eat chicken noodle soup, I feel connected to generations within my family who celebrated Sunday in this way, especially when there is a pot of it simmering for hours, which has you salivating all day.

The farming lifestyle may have been the best way to look at time blocking because they had a routine for everything. They had meals every day at the same time, and coffee time was a whole ritual. There was no rushing, no skipping breaks, just respecting the time you had to do work, then rest. Respecting the moment and the food being put in front of them. Respecting yourself and your time. **Plant your seeds and they will grow. You may not see the ripple effect, but it will be there. It will move into future generations. What if the seeds you plant are never for you to enjoy, but are for future generations?**

My son was watching *Berenstain Bears*, his favorite, and Sister planted an apple seed. She checked on it every day, but nothing was growing. She was getting impatient. She went back to school and the teacher asked if she had been watering it. "Yes," she said. Then she shared that it was an apple tree seed. The teacher laughed and said she would have to wait a long time. Instead, she could take one of his seeds. She replied, "No, thanks, I will wait." Her grandfather planted his apple tree calling it the "Fishing Tree." It is still there waiting for him when he goes fishing. She wanted that as well.

It got me thinking about how many things we or our ancestors plant that grow after our lifetime. Plant it and let it be. All we need is patience and no expectations. It will come when it does. Today, plant your seeds and wait. The apple trees will come, and you may even eat the fruit.

How was this land used? How did the people live? Since I was a child, this historical lens on life and happenings has intrigued me. I loved finding the similarities and differences between generations. It's for me to build empathy and leave space for past hardship, to better understand myself and my place in this ancestral picture. That is what I want to pass on to future generations.

On these trips back to ancestral lands, we learn who we are. You begin to connect all the pieces of your ancestors and what you want to bring to the equation for future generations. The more you understand what you contribute, the more it will make sense why you can provide it. To keep language and culture flourishing, we need to accept what it means to us. It's about leaving the door open for future generations for them to be able to see how they want to define themselves in all of this. You just have to leave the door open for them to want to peek in and see what works for them. Everyone gets to pick what works best for them, and they can mix and match. It's with their purpose leaving space for these messages that previous generations told to us at the dining table. Move between languages without losing the meaning in translating. Somewhere in this book, you'll find exactly what you need. It will be authentic to you.

We are the result of previous generations who took on risks, built skills, saved, generously gave, were persistent, and most importantly, survived. I am grateful that I am here because of all of them. I represent a human puzzle of all of them and their experiences. We continue to hold space for the next generations and those who come next.

When I got married, I put a braid in my hair because it is a symbol of youthful femininity. Then at midnight you officially become a woman and wife, so you undo your braid and your mother places a flowery headscarf on you as a symbol of womanhood and your new status as a wife. Now to me, braiding is the symbol of femininity, union, community, and of mind, body, and spirit coming together. Braid together wisdom to come together and be one.

Drying garlic, you braid it and hang it up to dry. It is lovely to look at and resembles a woman's braid. My grandmother worked hard for the majority of her days and life. The memory of her braiding looks different from the other tasks I saw her do. My family is filled with traditions and rural practices. In this journey of life, I am looking to mix the past traditions with what resonates with me. **Braiding traditions, ideas, and intuition together brings out the ancestral connection.** The beauty of the braid, the oneness.

Today is the guarantee. As you see the past and the future, the gift is today. It all makes sense because of today. It starts with the sunrise and ends with the sunset. What are you creating and appreciating from your day? I am grateful for the beginning and the end of the day—each day has so much to teach me. I am able to learn when I am present today and not attached to any other day. **Each day, as it comes to an end, ask yourself: what am I grateful for today?**

PLANT YOUR SEEDS

1. What can you start today?

_____

_____

_____

_____

2. Through reflection, what is something that has come up for you in this chapter?

_____

_____

_____

_____

_____

_____

3. How are you going to keep these big ideas top of mind every day?

_____

_____

_____

_____

_____

_____

4. What bigger project can you start today? Something that was on your mind but fear kept stopping you.

_____

_____

_____

_____

_____

_____

_____

_____

_____

_____

5. Why now? This is the best moment.

_____

_____

_____

_____

_____

_____

_____

_____

_____

YOUR TIME IS IMPORTANT

When my son turned five he said, "Mama, I don't want to die. I want to live on Earth forever. I am scared of going to Heaven alone."

It wasn't the conversation I thought we would be having on the day of his birthday. I woke up happy, finished my morning routine, and listened to a great episode of Super Soul Sunday with Phil Jackson, the Zen Master. Then I held my son and told him that it was okay to be scared. I told him no one has all the answers. He said he wants to come back after a couple of days in Heaven. We talked about reincarnation and how some people believe you come back but not to your current life. He liked that. He then proceeded to ask our immediate family if they wanted to come back too.

Maybe it's not about being scared of the end or lacking control but of knowing that you will have options. He felt complete after hearing all of this from me. He uses me as a sounding board to all of life's big questions, and I have the pleasure of pondering with him. The message I give him is also for me.

We were in Poland the first night, and as my oldest was falling asleep, he started crying heavily. He was crying so much, then he started screaming. He had so much fear and sadness, which was very unusual for him. He was crying because my husband was not there with us and he missed his dad. After a few more minutes, out of tiredness, he fell asleep. This happened again the next two nights. On that third night, I looked at him and said, "We do not get to be in Poland every day, it is a gift. We are seeing people we would not normally see. You've gotten to know your cousins that you never met. Tato (Dad) is in Canada. He is waiting for us. That won't change. All you have to do is enjoy today and the unique opportunity we have to be here."

He stopped crying after that. I knew I was speaking to myself too. It was the first trip that I was present and not thinking about what I was missing outside of the current moment. I heard people's stories about their truths and intuition. I got the privilege of learning something new about people I had known all my life.

My sister and I also bonded on this trip. Realizing the gift that was given to us to be here with our three boys and see our routine and every day from an outside lens. To step back from our ideas of reality, our expectations. To see the details that were not visible to us. It was in our routine that we got to appreciate the change in environment and context. Enjoy the food, conversations, new daily rhythm, and feel the love from family that was not around in our Canadian life.

* * *

Yesterday was a tragic and powerfully resilient day in North America: September 11, 2021. A day that calls in remembrance and the strength of community. The now adult children telling the stories of their parents who passed away during this tragedy, the spouses telling us the story of their day. There is a heaviness that is felt on that anniversary.

On this same day, in the morning, I received a message from my sister that my aunt had passed away. She was fighting her second battle with cancer. It all hit me—the permanence of death. It was the end of her earthly journey. A few weeks prior to this, I was reading a chapter of Brother David's book about death and he stated: "Death is the final, there is no more." He goes on to say that only when you truly understand death, can you comprehend life. Now that was a statement! It was the first time I heard a religious leader talk about death in a way that was not being "protected" by Heaven. I grew up religious, and this was the first death that I experienced that I did not allow Heaven to cloud or overtake the grieving. I called my mother-in-law, who already heard the news and was grieving. I don't know what she was saying and I don't think she heard me. We both cried together on this phone call, releasing all of it. I cried doing the laundry, the dishes, bathing the boys, and putting them to bed that day. I received a text from my friend: "Can I do anything for what you're feeling?"

As it has been recently, it was the right message at the right time, and I received it.

This also was after the first week of school and after my husband had received a positive Covid test. All four of us were self-isolating.

My emotions had been building for the last week. I was losing control of the big plans I made for myself, my business, my new roles at work, and my family. I planned a different beginning to the school year. It was spiraling out of my control, and I could feel it inside of me.

I knew I had to talk to my friend. A few minutes before her text, my Instagram hit 202 followers, I was following 20 people, and my book was to be published in 2022. All of these "2"s were jumping out from the page. Obviously, I needed to do some research on the number 2. It's tied to duality. What jumped at me: male/female, yes/no, left/right, yin/yang, and alive/dead. It was time for me to review my own peace and harmony.

I was ready to talk to my friend because she obviously knew something that I was missing. I poured out all the things: the stress, the grief, and the heaviness I was feeling in my heart. Behind my bedroom window, the leaves and branches were blowing around that evening, not looking very peaceful. As I told her this through the tears, she kindly listened and told me she had been having a lot of these conversations lately. People around her were wanting conversations that tied back to death. She told me about a colleague who was struggling with an ill spouse. He showed her the beauty of family connection, how he is taking care of his spouse. It brought her to tears. Prior to this day, I did not talk about death quite like this, in a grounded way. My friend listened to more of what I had to say and finally responded: "What if you were meant to take this week for rest and to spend it with your family?"

Hmm, I thought. What if this is exactly the week I needed to have? I told her she was right, and I left the talk with lightness. She made me see that my deadlines were self-made and that my November was going to be even better than I imagined for my company launch. I looked out to see the leaves stop moving from the night wind outside my bedroom window.

The first day my son took the bus, we were walking toward it when a playful and strong gust of wind came out from behind me. The wind moved the leaves and branches. It happily encircled me and my son. I did not notice the wind before or its movement. I did not feel it the way I felt it that day. It moved my soul, and I knew I was doing what I was meant to be doing that morning. It was going to be a good day. I came home smiling.

Also, in my despair and sadness, in my heaviness, another friend messaged me about a multigenerational project I had been intuitively shown to create. An opportunity to bring together people, cultures, and languages. We owe it to the people who cannot join us, to tie our souls together. This is something that I told a few of my friends a few months ago because the intuitive hit that came that day was compelling. It was bigger than me. It was while I was dancing with my sons to an instrumental Avicii that I imagined me yelling to a crowd. Welcoming them in multiple languages: Dzien dobry! Konnichiwa! Buenos días! It was for our ancestors and the people who could not join us. Tears collecting in my eyes, the beauty of one, of togetherness.

My friend's text wrote: "Tell me more about your project." She then sent a photo from the lands that her family was from. She was in Poland, driving to a wedding, through this land, and thinking about my project. It was beginning to take form, and she said if there was anything I needed help with, she was available. I was feeling heavy and sad, but there was someone who wanted to help me. I knew this was a message sent for me to take action and to understand it was easier than I thought.

"My soul is at peace here," she said.

"My soul is smiling," I replied.

After telling a few people about this multigenerational project, my favorite comment was when a previous colleague said, "It sounds like you have a plan."

My goal was taking form, and it was being manifested by the community. I knew this is the reason I was born—this was my purpose! It kept unfolding with every month because I was now seeing it take shape.

The next day, on Sunday, another friend who heard about our situation, messaged me: "If you need to talk, I am available."

After my coach taught me to receive from others, I had to keep receiving it. On Monday morning, we chatted. She said, "Remember, our coach says that you will have a dip right before your biggest success."

I had forgotten, but I knew she reminded me for a reason. This was my dip in my self-judgment, this was the "stuff" I needed to work through to get to the other side.

In the morning, we had a group coaching call when the coach talked about self-judgment right after I wrote my "I am . . ." statements. I understood my judgments that day. This week I felt like a failure as a being, mother, wife, and community member. When my son's class and bus got canceled, due to Covid, I felt like I failed to protect those around me from challenges. It was an unnecessary judgment of myself instead of appreciating the gift of time with myself and my family.

What was impressive about this week was that I was brought to tears instead of anger. My old self would have argued with my husband from the place of my challenges. It would have gotten heated. My new self went within and wanted to better understand my own struggle. Through all of this crying and despair, I was led to another conversation with my brother-in-law. He was able to continue conversations with various organizations to keep growing our business ideas. It came with ease. What I needed to do was give myself time to rest. All week I was in bed by 9:30 p.m. and journaling. I was following my routine. This was the last piece of news I needed to hear in order to move on and learn from the experience. I listened to the messages the right people left me so that I could be my best self.

I took the time that evening to work through an intuitive activity before my next course with my intuitive mentor. The activity was about learning how to ask my intuition questions. Here I was taking notes about the wind, birds, trees, leaves, and branches—I knew I was on the right track. I had another tool to add to my intuitive bucket: the wind. As always, I said, "Thank you, Universe, for showing me what

I need to do next. I release control and expectations of what will be. It is going to come at the right time. I am ready to live every day as if it were my last. I am moving into accepting messages I'm receiving daily. I promise to listen with my ears, eyes, and soul. I will listen to the push and pulls of my intuition."

> "IF YOU HAVE FAITH EVEN AS SMALL AS A MUS-TARD SEED, YOU CAN SAY TO THIS MOUNTAIN, 'MOVE FROM HERE TO THERE,' AND IT WOULD MOVE. NOTHING WOULD BE IMPOSSIBLE."
>
> **—Matthew 17:20**

Last year, I wrote a letter to myself. To the future me as if everything was already accomplished. I truly felt like I was there and this was my life:

My life as a writer, traveling with my family and giving myself time to create. In Costa Rica, South of France, Italy, Greece, Madagascar, Poland, Japan, and New Zealand. Finding places to be creative, finding places to find a narrative, while dreaming big. I dream big and make time for these creative juices.

> "I AM RESPONSIBLE FOR MY LIFE, FOR MY FEELINGS, FOR MY PERSONAL GROWTH, AND FOR EVERY RESULT I GET."
>
> **—Bob Proctor**

When I received intuitive hits—as I got them often enough—my faith and belief in the unknown increased. I started feeling this pull, and I started trusting that I would be led somewhere better and learn what I needed to from the new situation. My faith unraveled with my morning self-work and finding gratitude in the small moments. Seeing the potency in the small experiences like walking in nature, planting flowers, washing dishes, writing, and painting. These moments show you the power of your mind and heart to be in the task you are doing and how important your faith is on this journey.

PHOENIX

In those moments of loss
Those moments of true sadness, complete loss
Can we build from the ashes?
Grow and develop into something bigger. Something more
Be the phoenix of your life, of your experiences
Only then when we are above those ashes do we truly know
what we are capable of.

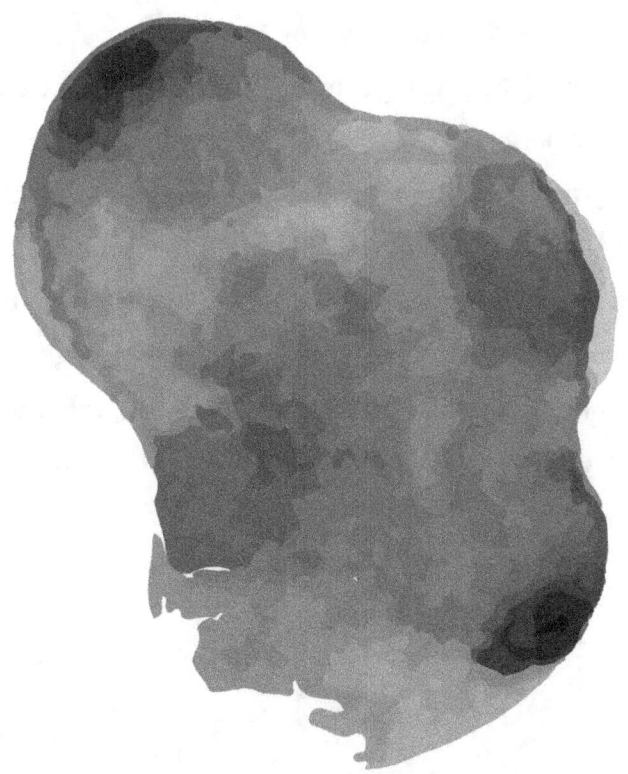

My sister came over to my house in the fall of 2020 and started crying. She was six weeks pregnant and had been trying for a year and a half at that point. She had just come from her fertility clinic appointment where the ultrasound had shown that based on the fetus's growth, she would miscarry in the next few weeks. That morning, we held each other and cried—from our souls. My arms were there for love and support. After we stopped, my sister accepted her reality, and I saw her transform like a phoenix. There was so much beauty and strength to what I saw in her at that moment. My sister was unstoppable. She was bigger than any situation that came her way. I still feel so much gratitude that she invited me into her fertility journey because I got to see this moment of transformation. I saw her transform before my eyes.

In the book *The Art of Gathering*, author Priya Parker shares a story about her mother organizing a gathering for her with her close aunts when she first got her period. It was to celebrate her becoming a woman, and she received various gifts to mark the occasion. I thought back to my own experience as a young woman when I got my period and being gifted red roses. The sign of womanhood. An acknowledgment of changes in my body, a transformation. The more I've gotten to experience the power of womanhood and motherhood, the more grateful I am to be a woman with all the complexities that come with it.

BABY SHOWER LOVE LETTER TO MY SISTER

I have been given a gift this year during the various lockdowns. I got to spend more time talking and chatting with you than ever before. I think we started talking three or four times a day.

Today, we are here to celebrate you becoming a mother and this baby. I wanted to write you a love letter because I have fallen in love with you more and more over the course of your journey of motherhood. Your journey to motherhood has been two years, four months so far. I remember when I got my positive pregnancy test with Vinny and called you almost immediately to share the news. We started chatting about having kids close together. How exciting, cousins only a few months apart. It wasn't exactly how you and I envisioned it from there.

I am sincerely thankful to you for sharing your journey with me. You included me in every step. Throughout all of this, I have seen you transform as a woman and as a being. There are moments in your journey that will forever be stamped in my mind. In September of 2020, you and Andrij told us you were pregnant. What a joy I felt; it took over my whole body and led to a downpouring of tears! Then the day you came over in the fall of 2020 to tell me that the tests at the clinic did not look good. That you would miscarry in the next couple of weeks. My arms and heart grew that day holding you. Seeing you rise from the ashes. You rose into this phoenix. I cannot explain what I saw that day. But it was the biggest version of you I have ever seen. You became more than your 4'11" being.

I read this quote and thought about you: "The deeper sorrow carves into your being, the more joy you can contain." You told us in January 2021 that you were pregnant again. We were all feeling cautious, not knowing what to say or do so we all waited. One morning I called you and asked how you were doing. You said the morning sickness was getting worse. You then went on to explain your gratitude practice. As you were going through this, you would say to yourself how grateful you were to be pregnant. Yet another conversation that changed me. You have shown me that from deep grief can come deep joy.

Throughout all of this, you have been surrounded by unconditional love and support. From your "fertility squad" to your family to your friends to your piano students' moms. At the beginning of the pregnancy, you were only a month pregnant, but the morning sickness got so bad you had to share the pregnancy earlier with a few of the students' moms. You received an outpouring of love and support, so many kind words came your way. The power of womanhood.

Now a love note for Ciocia Lesia! You are always there. No matter what. You are there for school concerts, birthdays, achievements. My kids think of you as their constant. Yelling "I love you" when you leave, knocking on the window for the goodbyes, then you still drive by for final blow away kisses. You have given your heart to them, no wonder they love you so. I promise to take my new role as an aunt as seriously as you do.

Our cousin in her wedding vows included that everything they do will be rooted in love as they were standing in the Royal Botanical Gardens with a never-ending green backdrop and under a tree. As I am thinking about this, that is the kind of aunt I want to be. Rooted in love. My arms and heart will be available to your child. I will be there for absolutely every moment. I will be the cheerleader, the support, the unconditional love. Thank you for showing me the way to aunthood.

It has been a privilege to walk beside you in this journey of motherhood. To hold your hand. When we were growing up, you said that you learned so much from me. That you looked up to me. This year, I definitely look up to you and who you are. Lesh, there are things you have shown me over the last two years that are etched into my heart forever. Thank you for everything you have shared with me; you've shown me the true meaning of motherhood.

When my son was born, I wrote him a letter, which I wanted to turn into a book for him. I wrote it in a notebook that I now use as a morning journal. This was supposed to be the beginning of a personal book for him. I want to share it here:

Happy eighteenth birthday. I hope this birthday is very special, the beginning of adulthood. I hope that you make the time to enjoy not only today or this year but the journey of adulthood. Adulthood is a delightful stage in life. A time to create true independence, your purpose, passions, love, empathy, and to explore the unknown. I hope that whatever experiences or opportunities come your way, you pick the one that gives you passion. Leads you to your goals.

I'm writing this book for you because I don't know where I'll be for your eighteenth birthday, but I know I'll be thinking of you and wishing you the most beautiful things in life. As I begin to write, you are sixteen weeks old. I will be writing this in parts and adding to it as we go through life and we grow together. I don't want to forget to say something important. This is why I am doing this from now until your eighteenth birthday.

As your mother, I am writing this because I love you and want to share some advice and experiences through my lens. I'm currently twenty-seven and have some life experience. By the time you are eighteen, I'll be forty-five. Hopefully, I'll have life figured out a little bit more. You're going to be so big, just thinking about it gets me teared up.

The goal of this book is to share what I think is the most important to have in life. After you go through your journey, you will make your own decision. Make sure, whatever you choose leads you to the life path you want to be on. That it brings you joy.

Remember, I am so happy that your father and I chose to have you. That we could have children because I never knew

I could love someone this much and in this way. I love you! You mean the world to me. Happy eighteenth birthday!

Note, I marked eighteen emotions and experiences I think are most important to have in life. It will be written in different fonts because I'm writing it as we go through life. Enjoy!

On that day, I wrote: family, compromise, and purpose. As I write this book, I think these are still true to this day.

PLANT YOUR SEEDS

1. With your one life, what do you want?

_____

_____

_____

_____

_____

_____

2. What are the ten things you are most grateful for right now?

_____

_____

_____

_____

_____

_____

3. How can you make more time for rest?

_____

_____

_____

_____

_____

_____

4. How can you make more time for reflection?

_____
_____
_____
_____
_____
_____
_____
_____
_____

5. How does intuition show you your truth?

_____
_____
_____
_____
_____
_____
_____
_____
_____
_____

CONCLUSION

EMBRACE THE UNKNOWN

The most powerful year of my life was when I turned my life into quarters. I was able to release all pressure and lean into all of these ideas. It did not matter how I worked through these ideas, they just had to be top of mind. Every quarter I would write it on my bathroom wall as a daily reminder. I picked out a word; I allowed myself to discover more than ever before. I regularly journaled about these feelings and ideas. Each quarter highlighted a need that I felt inspired for myself: Discovery, Abundance, Implementation, and Level Up.

Remember when my son told me he thought there should be pictures in my book? That was my inspiration. I included space for you to write. Throughout this book, I hope you make the time to go back to these words and keep adding more. Create when you're inspired. Then keep creating, it will move you into even more intuitive work.

One night as I was going to sleep, an infinity sign flashed in my mind over and over again. The past, the present, and the future were all flowing through me. I felt I was standing in the center and this whole time they flowed through me. I hold space for all the stories, life, and existence that is there. I hold the key to all of it. It is already inside of me.

The trip to Poland for my grandmother's funeral rooted our family. My oldest was able to visit with intrigue—his family, his background, and the country of his ancestors. He wanted to learn more. Over the course of the month, there were a lot of questions. He also saw how the past, present, and future flowed through him.

He got to meet his last two great-grandparents and see how my maternal grandfather needed support with walking, eating, and bathing. In the immigrant story, one generation usually skips over seeing this aging in front of their eyes. When we met my husband's grandmother, he couldn't believe it. He kept saying, "Great-grandma can do everything by herself. She can eat, walk, work, and can even drive a car!" That last part wasn't true, but he assumed from all the other independent tasks. He celebrated her abilities, her strength.

I got to hear about their stories and see the youngest generation interact with them. It was coming full circle, and I got to be in the rooted middle. They would run around her, watch TV on her bed, and eat in her room—they wanted to be beside her.

One evening, I was sitting with my aunt and cousin, and we were discussing familial intuition and how the women used it in the past to heal and medicate with local herbs. They knew what was happening in the body and what was needed. We started talking about the projects we have dreamed up for our familial land and the exciting opportunities that were coming to the village in the next couple of years. There was positive energy around all of this. We were ready to create and put those ideas into form. We all left that conversation with intention—seeds were planted that night.

Throughout the trip to Poland, I kept waking up in the morning and feeling an unrest. Then with each day I kept feeling soldiers gathering on the edge of the mountain. They kept coming. I understood that the unrest around Ukraine's border with the surrounding Russian troops was about to get violent and Poland would be impacted. We went to the gravesite of my grandfather and lit a candle. I looked at the sky and felt it in the ground, it was just around the corner. I could feel it. That night I looked at my sister and asked her if she was feeling anything in this area. She said it was time for us to leave. We rebooked our flight two days earlier, and later that week, the Russian troops crossed the Ukrainian border.

"ULTIMATELY, WE HAVE ONE MORAL DUTY
TO RECLAIM LARGE AREAS OF PEACE IN
OURSELVES, MORE AND MORE PEACE, AND
TO REFLECT IT TOWARD OTHERS. AND THE
MORE PEACE THERE IS IN US, THE MORE PEACE
THERE WILL BE IN OUR TROUBLED WORLD."

—Etty Hillesum

As we entered that airport, on the way back home, we knew we might not be back for a while. We felt this goodbye to the land, to the village, and felt the calm in us. Yes, we had three little kids with us, and yes, we were sweating from moving all our belongings, but there was calm. We felt absolutely grateful to our grandmother that she passed away at the right time for us to easily come into the country and leave easily as well. She gave us many gifts on this trip. She gave us time, appreciation of our land and multigenerational projects, seed planting for future generations, a welcoming family, and love for our culture and language, particularly for the younger generation. She helped us find ourselves and tied us back to our land. I hadn't been back for the last seven and a half years. When I landed there, I appreciated how much I changed in that time as I became a mother (twice). I grew so much with my self-work that I was able to see the lasting meaning of our visit for both myself and my sons. I promised myself it wouldn't take me that long to return.

I will be back soon because this is only the beginning. We have many more things to create. The people that I will create with are here, and all the energy of past generations lives on here in the mountains, in the homes, in the cemetery. They see us and they show us the paths available to us. They see the opportunity for growth and will create the possibility for all of this. We are ready to bring our big ideas to life, one day at a time. Thank you, Baba! You have changed my life and planted seeds and ideas in me that cannot be unseen. I will create these talents that I have rediscovered.

Why this book? Why now? Why not later when I figure it all out and get to look back instead of forward? Because life is a work in progress. We are constantly growing, showing, exploring, discovering. Why not me! **The door that opens invites someone to walk through, why not me?** I receive all the gifts when I connect with my intuition. The gifts keep presenting themselves to me, they fall on my lap.

What I want you to embrace from this book is how life impacts you, and for you to create space to be present, to understand who you are and what you bring to life. When you know who you are, you know what you bring to the next generation, and they get to gain. Everyone around you will grow when your cup is filled. Take the time to slow down by remembering and practicing the three ways of authentically connecting to yourself:

1. Being rooted in yourself by being you, the deep down you.
2. Living a life of creation by making time to create and discover.
3. Remembering you are alive, use your time wisely.

There is something that gets planted in all of us for generations and shows up in us. It comes out when we are ready. Our families have talents, passion, and abilities that are a gift. It is time to present it. Something will grow out of all of this, and it will be bigger than any one person or one generation. It is with the future in mind, by living in the present, and remembering the gifts of the past. Remember who you are in this one beautifully wild life. There are seeds you are planting now that may not grow until future generations. Release expectations and allow your growth to take place.

Make space for fullness and abundance in what you do every day. We are on this journey for a long time—all you have to do is begin. For instance, having morning meditation sessions can be the beginning of fullness and abundance in your life. When you purposefully wake up and act joyfully in the morning, you could fill your cup by 9 a.m. When you invest time in yourself, you draw in positive energy, which reminds you to think bigger than you thought before. The intention will lead to implementation and activating goodness for yourself. So does taking the time to write out these goals, ideas, intention, and gratitude. The words and ideas will lead into making things exist and take form.

We do not need to know what the end product is; for example, for creativity you can start sketching and end up painting. All of these abilities are already sitting inside you—you have to begin using them to see what you are capable of. I don't need to know what the end product is or what it will look like, the feeling or nudge will tell me when I reach it. You will feel grounded with yourself.

How and where do I even start? That is a question I hear often. Start by writing down all the feelings you want to experience. Buy a sketchbook and notebook, start by writing or drawing it all down. My goal is to hold space for people and to see borderless creativity. I plant seeds of authenticity in ourselves. To build authentic families and communities. No one has these answers except for you. You will find the right ones along the way. **The journey is a lifetime, and you already have what you need within yourself**.

2022: I've never been more excited about a year and started writing the date with such ease. I was already writing the date before the year started. I was in 2022 before it even came. I decided this was going to be my year. The year was given to me and I would receive. Thank you in all that is offered to me, in the small moments of the daily happenings. Make every year yours!

I moved my furniture around on the balcony and in the backyard. Made the balcony for the kids and the backyard for more sit-down gatherings while we barbeque. After a few weeks of setting this up, it came to me that this was a place for my ancestors to sit and enjoy. For them to exchange stories. I will benefit, I will learn.

During a group intuitive session, I had a nudge that the land I currently live on wanted to tell me something. In my vision, I felt the heat right away. It was a huge, violent fire. I was wearing a long black embroidered dress. I walked up to this fire and hugged it. Then paused to kiss it. Immediately, it sucked me in through a long ashy tunnel to the depths of the Earth. I went to the cold and dark bottom. Then it sucked me back up and I ran my hand along the ashy tunnel. As I did, grass, moss, and colorful flowers appeared. There was growth. The land was healed.

Here I am! A woman who thought it was about the corporate climb, the success roller coaster. When really I needed to activate my fullest self and start seeing the strength in me, outside of all of these achievements. It is about creating, using imagination, releasing control, and seeing there is more. **It is already here—you just have to crack it open!**

I made French toast a couple of days ago. I made it from a different emotional space than usual. I made it for myself. I saw the extra bread and knew that this was what I wanted to make. The emotions were so strong. My family benefited from this experience, but I made it for myself first. This was a philosophical French toast. I didn't need any compliments or gratitude. I only needed my fullness, my satisfaction. Pleasure created by me.

I do things for my kids, of course. However, on the days I feel full and joy with layers of gratitude, I do it for myself first. It is not about spending money or going somewhere. It has always been right inside of me. Right HERE!

My sister, who has been doing a lot of self-work, was saying she couldn't wait to travel after the pandemic lockdowns and listed all of the places she wants to go to. I told her what she is looking for is not there. What she was running from was inside of her, the tired, the exhausted, the changes as a new mom, the new relationships, and the new reality. The next day, we chatted again, and she said that initially she was irritated by my comment even though she knew it came from a place of love and support. She wanted to hear what a great idea it was and that she should buy those tickets, while I asked her to open up emotionally.

My boys made me visualize there is so much more to life than just a career. It's everything you do outside of work and who you choose to be. It's the kitchen dance parties, seasonal crafts, gingerbread house making, piano playing, bathtime, races to be first, dinner chats, daily walks, car/truck watching, excitement when guests come over, helping Baba and Dido fix a fence, going sledding, seeing the first snow (my favorite experience every year), raking the leaves, hugging the Paw Patrol outdoor Christmas decoration, summer reading, blowing out candles on a cake, surprising someone, chasing each other around the house, throwing clothing out of the hamper with a smile.

Thank you for helping me slow down and appreciate the moments. Now I know, life is a series of fortunate and unfortunate events, and you choose which to put more focus on. **I hope you stop and celebrate the small fortunate events because they are more significant than you think.**

I am, I am, I am. I live authentically because I am everything and nothing. I am all of these things and none of these things. I can have it all and enjoy today. **Be you! Be BOLDLY you! You are already who you want to be.** It has been inside of you this whole time. Everything you want is just outside of the fear you feel inside of your body. Don't let it stop you. There is only goodness on the other side. Come and see!

HOME

I am home
It is a place with no front door
No windows or roof.
It is a place for me but not purchased by me
It is mine deep down.
Home is not tied to a structure, a specific country, or tied to citizenship
It is tied to a feeling that pulls, pulls you toward it.
You know when you get there because you feel grateful
You feel whole
Absolute fullness, it warms your soul.
This is exactly where you were meant to be
Welcome home! It has been here all along, inside of you.

RESOURCES

Listed in alphabetical order:

Joan Chittister, *In the Heart of the Temple*, 2004

Maureen Gaffney, *Your One Wild and Precious Life: An Inspiring Guide to Becoming Your Best Self At Any Age*, 2019

Natalia Harhaj, www.nataliaharhaj.com

Etty Hillesum, *Etty Hillesum: An Interrupted Life and Letters from Westerbork*, 1996

Eddie Jaku, *The Happiest Man on Earth*, 2020

Hina Khan, www.hinakhan.ca

Dee Montie, www.deemontie.com

Barack Obama, *Dreams from My Father*, 2004

Priya Parker, *The Art of Gathering*, 2020

Michelle Pena, www.michellepena.ca

Bob Proctor, www.proctorgallagherinstitute.com

Taras Shevchenko, www.shevchenko.ca

Tosha Silver, *Outrageous Openness: Letting the Divine Take the Lead*, 2011

Brother David Steindl-Rast, *Common Sense Spirituality: The Essential Wisdom of David Steindl-Rast*, 2008

Elie Wiesel, "Conversations with Oprah: Elie Wiesel," 1993

Oprah Winfrey, www.oprah.com/app/super-soul-sunday

ACKNOWLEDGMENTS

Thank you to my husband and best friend, Lubo, who makes space for all of my big ideas. I appreciate all your support and that you saw my creativity before I did. To my boys, Jeremy and Vincent, who have humbled me as a mother and continue to show me the true meaning of life every day. You are the reason this book was even possible. You planted so many seeds for me.

I am forever grateful to my sister and Mama, Lesia and Anna, who were always ready to read the newest version of this book. With their excitement, they motivate me to run with all the projects and ideas in my head. I appreciate all your feedback and the time you devoted to this project. Ivasyk, Adrian, and Andrew, thank you for exploring these stories with me; your ears were always open. To Maria, Stefan, and Alejandra, who took care of my boys as deadlines got closer. You gave me peace of mind so I could keep writing. Tato, thank you for helping me with my house projects as I was creating the creative spaces, your support got me to the end product.

To the hype squad of women around me, who support me with regular encouragement, thank you! This includes: Dominika, Olena, Sonya, Lidia, Anna, Fazzy, Cathy, Andriana, Marianka, Darya, Elle, Christina, Kristina, Rhea, Adriana, Anita, Irene, Sophia, Oresta, Halyna, Tanya, Dayna, Andrea, Joey, and Cousin. You all helped me take my creativity to the next level. Your kind words through this project were appreciated.

The group who supports my brand and building my dreams even bigger: Kristina and Maria. Thank you for making sure I stay true to my deadlines and stay focused on the end goal.

To the Alair team, Andrew, Evelynn, Andrew, and Mike. Thank you for your kind words and support.

To my ancestors, who have passed down familial stories, that are a part of each of us. I appreciate that our stories are weaving together and we all plant seeds for the future. Together, we have a powerful message. Together, we can have an impact. Together, we stay focused on something bigger than ourselves. To all of our family in Poland, who make space and time for us when we visit. You show us all the changes and excitement that goes on. We always love seeing you.

To all the people who have seen or joined me on this journey, I always appreciate an intense chat.

Lastly, to all the Ukrainians who are fighting for something bigger than themselves. We are forever grateful for what you do to protect the land. To fight for the freedom to practice culture, religion, and language. From the bottom of my heart, thank you. Слава Україні! Героям Слава!

YGTMedia Co. is a blended boutique publishing house for mission-driven humans. We help seasoned and emerging authors "birth their brain babies" through a supportive and collaborative approach. Specializing in narrative nonfiction and adult and children's empowerment books, we believe that words can change the world, and we intend to do so one book at a time.

🌐 ygtmedia.co/publishing

📷 @ygtmedia.co

𝐟 @ygtmedia.co

www.ingramcontent.com/pod-product-compliance
Lightning Source LLC
Chambersburg PA
CBHW061148120626
46546CB00005B/1968